BATTLE OF BRITAIN MEMORIAL FLIGHT

MEMORIAL FLIGHT

ROYAL AIR FORCE

LEST WE FORGET

Midland Publishing
Limited

The Battle of Britain
MEMORIAL FLIGHT

Bill Taylor

© 1995 Bill Taylor

Design concept and layout
© Midland Publishing Limited and
Stephen Thompson Associates

Published by
Midland Publishing Limited
24 The Hollow, Earl Shilton
Leicester, LE9 7NA
England

ISBN 1 85780 027 3

Printed in England by
The Alden Press
Oxford

Front cover: **For the 1994 display season, Spit-fire Mk.IIA P7350 was repainted in the colours of 72 Squadron and marked 'Enniskillen', to represent an aircraft funded by the** *Belfast Telegraph* **Spitfire Fund. With P7350 is Spitfire Mk.VB AB910, carrying the codes 'AE-H' of 402 (RCAF) Squadron, overpainted with the black and white fuselage bands applied to all Allied aircraft on D-Day.** BBMF

Rear cover, top: **Spitfire Mk.IIA P7350 photographed from the mid-upper turret of the Lancaster during a positioning flight on 18th May 1980.** C F E Smedley

Rear cover, centre: **Newly repainted in the colours of 9 Squadron, Lancaster PA474 gleams in the spring sunshine of early 1994 on its return to Coningsby following major servicing at St Athan.** BBMF

Rear cover, bottom: **Wearing the distinctive matt black colour scheme carried by night fighters and the markings of 85 Squadron, Hurricane Mk.IIC LF363 sits on the grass awaiting its display slot during Coningsby's annual air show on 14th June 1986.** Author

Half title page: **The BBMF badge.**
Courtesy of the Flight and Crown Copyright.

Title page: **The whole of the BBMF took to the air together during 1990 to mark the 50th anniversary of the Battle of Britain. Lancaster PA474 is followed by Hurricane Mk.IICs LF363 'GN-A' and PZ865 'RF-U'; Spitfire Mk.IIA P7350 'UO-T'; Spitfire Mk.VB AB910 'EB-J'; Spitfire Mk.XIXs PM631 'N', PS853 'C' and PS915 (uncoded). By 1995 every aircraft in this formation was at least 50 years old.** British Aerospace via BBMF

RAF PICTORIAL

FOREWORD

By Air Chief Marshal Sir Michael Alcock
KBE CB DSC CEng FIMechE FRAeS RAF
Air Officer Commanding-in-Chief
Air Member for Logistics and Chief Engineer
Headquarters Logistics Command

It is now fifty years since the end of the Second World War and at the many commemorative events held to mark the occasion the Royal Air Force contingent has been led by the Battle of Britain Memorial Flight. The historical significance of the Flight lies in its role as a living tribute to the many thousands of Royal Air Force personnel who gave their lives during that now distant conflict, especially those lost during the Battle of Britain and the bomber offensive.

For the Royal Air Force of today, however, the Battle of Britain Memorial Flight fills a vital role in projecting an image of the achievements of its people in the past and of the standards and dedication required of those who form its future. The Flight serves as an inspiration to young and old alike, aiding the Royal Air Force in its recruiting task and helping the general public understand the role of the armed forces. Because these historic aircraft are maintained in flying condition, the Royal Air Force has the ability to reach a wide audience and the many hundreds of requests for aircraft to appear at functions other than major air displays bears testament to the place the Battle of Britain Memorial Flight holds in the heart of the community.

In this work, Group Captain Bill Taylor has assembled a wealth of information and photographs which chart the history both of the Flight and its aircraft and the important work that goes on behind the scenes to maintain the aircraft and to plan the extensive annual flying programme. Both in words and pictures, the author has captured the spirit of what the Battle of Britain Memorial Flight means to so many people.

Sir Michael Alcock

INTRODUCTION

The present-day Royal Air Force contains many units which are unique in their task and role, but none more so than the Battle of Britain Memorial Flight (BBMF), based at Coningsby in Lincolnshire. Superficially, one might be tempted to view the Flight as just another airshow attraction, but behind that gleaming facade there is a purpose which has its roots deep in the heart of the nation – to act as a living memorial which allows both the Royal Air Force and the general public to articulate a debt of gratitude to an earlier generation.

The Flight's historic significance to the nation is self-evident, symbolising the victory won in the Battle of Britain and offering a living tribute to the thousands of RAF personnel who lost their lives in the Second World War – some 56,000 aircrew died in Bomber Command alone. More than this, the Flight is also a living tribute to the designers and the aircraft industry that provided the RAF with the means to earn its place in history.

Whilst there might be strong emotional ties to the RAF, in these days of stringent Government scrutiny of all aspects of expenditure, the Flight must also have a clear military purpose relevant to the needs of a modern high-technology air force if there is to be any justification for its continued existence. Clearly, the Flight's primary remit is to aid the RAF in its public relations and recruiting, and to project defence in the public eye. The achievements of the RAF over many years remain etched in the mind of the public, both young and old. When seen in flight the aircraft of the BBMF bring to mind the valour and sacrifice demanded of those serving in the RAF, not only in the past but also today. If the historic aircraft of the Flight were to become only static museum pieces they would be seen by just a minute fraction of the audience reached by the airworthy aircraft each year. Interestingly, the Flight's hangar at Coningsby is the only part of the modern RAF that the general public may visit on a day-to-day basis.

The aim of this short work is to try to lift the lid a little on what the BBMF is and how it has evolved into a national institution. Just how are the Flight's historic aircraft kept airworthy and how are they sustained for the benefit of future generations? What markings have the aircraft carried and what was their significance? If it answers questions such as these, then the book will have achieved its aim. However, in doing so, I should point out that the views expressed are my own and do not necessarily reflect official policy.

As I carried out my research it became clear that something very significant lay behind the professional display of historic aircraft presented by the RAF at so many air shows and other events. Perhaps it is that the BBMF is the living embodiment of the spirit and heritage of the RAF. The Flight is certainly a source of justifiable national pride in the skills of our aircraft designers and builders and in the valour and sacrifice of a generation.

Acknowledgements

To complete this tribute to the Battle of Britain Memorial Flight, I have relied heavily on the help of many people. Foremost of these must of course be the staff of the Flight itself, including Squadron Leaders Andy Tomalin and Rick Groombridge, but especially the groundcrew under Warrant Officers Barry Sears and Len Sutton. Access to primary research material was aided by Graham Day, Peter Singleton and Steve Clark in the Air Historical Branch (RAF), whilst Squadron Leader David Blythe-Brook's years of experience on the RAF's Historic Aircraft Committee proved invaluable in sorting many of the facts from previously published information. Major organisations were also of considerable help: including the photographic departments of British Aerospace at Dunsfold and Warton; Dorothy Hill, Paul Churcher and Bob Fry at Cranfield University; and Tim Routsis and Clive Denney at Historic Flying Limited.

Many individuals were also kind enough to provide help, either in the form of information or photographs: John Armond; Peter R Arnold; Tim Badham; Phil Butler; Ray Coulson; John Folkes; Neville Franklin; Peter Green; Steve Hague; Mike Hodgson; Leslie Hunt; Frank Mason; Brian Pickering; Paddy Porter; Peter Pountney; Bruce Robertson; Robert Rudhall; Oscar Smedley; John Smith; and Andy Thomas.

Lastly, I must thank the team at Midland, especially Neil Lewis, Chris Salter, new recruit Ken Ellis and designer Steve Thompson, who between them have translated a rudimentary manuscript and a bundle of photographs into a product of which I am proud.

Bill Taylor
Friskney, Lincolnshire
July 1995

With the end of the war in Europe in May 1945, followed by the capitulation of Japan some three months later, the British public was keen for life to return to normal. The thousands of men and women enlisted in the armed forces wanted to be demobilised as soon as possible so that they could return to their wives, husbands, families and former jobs, or start the search for new employment. However, the years of war had wrought much change, and the heavy bombing attacks on the British Isles, especially the bombing of London, were still fresh in the mind of the public.

Whilst it was hard to forget the horrors of war, it was also difficult to forget the efforts of that valiant band of fighter pilots who had done so much to stave off the threat of invasion in that far-off summer of 1940. It was therefore fitting that the success of the Battle of Britain should be commemorated on 15th September each year by a flypast of RAF aircraft over London, led by a Hawker Hurricane and a Supermarine Spitfire. For the first such flypast in 1945 it was a quite straightforward matter to obtain the aircraft necessary to mount the flypast, and whilst the specific format changed from year to year, the availability of a Hurricane and a Spitfire was not at first a problem. However, the Hurricane was quickly withdrawn from service until, by mid-1950, the RAF had just one airworthy example remaining, Mk.IIC, LF363, which was on the strength of the Station Flight at Thorney Island, Sussex, and

kept airworthy to mount the annual flypast. (County names are given as those in use at the time.)

Hurricane Mk.IIC LF363

Built at Langley, Buckinghamshire, as a Mk.IIC, LF363 first flew on 1st January 1944, and was ferried to 5 Maintenance Unit (MU), Kemble, Gloucestershire, on the 28th. Its operational career began on 30th March when it was ferried to 63 Squadron at Turnhouse, Midlothian, moving two months later, on 23rd May, to 309 (Polish) Squadron at Drem, East Lothian. It is known that LF363 carried out at least 16 operational sorties with 309 Squadron before going to 22 MU, Silloth, Cumberland, on 1st November 1944. Records show that the following day it returned to 63 Squadron, before going to 26 Squadron on 30th November and returning

to 22 MU on 5th January 1945. On 15th April, LF363 moved to 62 Operational Training Unit (OTU) at Ouston, Durham, returning to 22 MU on 13th June, before going to Middle Wallop, Hampshire, on 28th August. The period spent at Middle Wallop is somewhat uncertain and LF363's duties during this period are unclear. However, its records show that it was struck off charge on 21st June 1947, but little more than two months later, on 14th August, it was taken on charge again at Middle Wallop. On 19th February 1948, LF363 was further transferred to the Thorney Island Station Flight.

Deep maintenance work was in the offing for the lone Hurricane on 30th October, when it was transferred to 41 Group, Maintenance Command, for major servicing. This was carried out by Hawkers at Langley, and the aircraft returned to Thorney Island

LF363 parked in front of Thorney Island's bomb-damaged hangar in 1948.
Peter Green collection

on completion of the work on 8th January 1949, where it suffered a wheels-up landing due to the unfamiliarity of the pilot with the Hurricane – he was making his first flight in the type. The groundcrew at Thorney Island put in considerable work to repair the aircraft and the records show that LF363 then joined the Station Flight at Odiham, Hampshire, on 26th June, before returning to Thorney Island on 22nd September. With

the transfer of Thorney Island from Fighter Command to Flying Training Command on 15th May 1950, the station's fighter squadrons were moved to Waterbeach, Cambridgeshire, and LF363 went with them. However, during a sortie by a 63 Squadron pilot on 1st October 1953, LF363 was slightly damaged when its canopy detached during flight, although it was quickly repaired once a replacement had been found. After further flying from Waterbeach, on 30th September 1955, LF363 was again sent to Hawkers at Langley for major servicing, emerging some nine months later in a pristine silver colour scheme. Collected from Langley on 28th June 1956, Wing Com-

mander Peter Thompson DFC flew LF363 to Biggin Hill, Kent, from where it mounted the annual London flypast in September.

Temperature and Humidity Flight
Having established the practice that the annual flypast over London should be led by a Hurricane and Spitfire, there was a widely held determination within the RAF to ensure that the means to commemorate the Battle of Britain in the most appropriate manner possible should be retained. By 1957 the end of Spitfire operations by the RAF was imminent, prompting the idea that a special flight should be formed around these historic aircraft to act as a memorial to

After being refurbished by Hawker at Langley, LF363 was in pristine condition.
Francis K Mason

'The Few' and to the RAF's greatest Battle Honour, and which could provide the Hurricane and Spitfire to lead the annual flypast over London.

The spur to this idea was the decision to withdraw the three Spitfire Mk.XIXs of the Temperature and Humidity Flight at Woodvale, Lancashire, in June 1957. This unique unit had formed at Hooton Park, Cheshire, in April 1951 and was universally referred to as the 'THUM' Flight. It commenced operations on 1st May, its task being to make daily ascents to 30,000 ft recording data on meteorological conditions. After each ascent, the aircraft landed at Liverpool Airport (otherwise known as Speke) where the data was analysed and sent to the Central Forecasting Office at Dunstable, Bedfordshire, for onward transmission throughout the world. The task was assumed on contract by Belfast-based Short Brothers and Harland, and the unit moved to Woodvale on 13th July. There were several reasons for the Spitfire Mk.XIX being chosen for the THUM Flight's work, especially its large internal fuel capacity giving it a duration of some four hours, its pressurised cockpit which made it relatively comfortable for high altitude flying, and its stability, which made it an ideal observation platform. The aircraft allocated to the Flight included PM549 (crashed 4th May 1952), PM631, PM652 (crashed 4th March 1954), PS853 and PS915, all of which were specially modified for their new role at 9 MU, Cosford, Shropshire, and provided excellent and generally reliable service throughout their days with the THUM Flight.

However, by 1956 spares for the Spitfires were becoming harder to find and the search began for a replacement aircraft, the de Havilland Mosquito Mk.35 eventually being chosen. The last operational ascent by a Spitfire of the THUM Flight, indeed, of the RAF, was flown on 10th June 1957, by PS853 some 21 years after the first flight of the prototype Spitfire. The event was marked by a presentation ceremony at Woodvale and on the 12th June an attempt was made to fly all three aircraft to Duxford, Cambridgeshire, and return them to RAF charge. However, PS915 refused to start, PM631 took off but suffered radio failure and landed again, whilst PS853 took off, but landed again with engine trouble which resulted in it running off the runway and tipping onto its nose. The aircraft were quickly repaired, and PM631 and PS915 flew to Duxford on 14th June, followed by PS853 on the 26th.

Formation of the Flight
Just two weeks later, on 11th July, the three Spitfires left Duxford accompanied by three Gloster Javelins and three Hawker Hunters to fly to Biggin Hill, piloted by a trio of distinguished pilots; Group Captain J E 'Johnny' Johnson, Group Captain James Rankin and Wing Commander Peter Thompson. On arrival at Biggin Hill, the aircraft joined

Having made an ascent to take meteorological readings, PS915 of the THUM Flight keeps its engine running whilst the details are handed over at Liverpool's Speke Airport on 4th September 1954.

Engine ground runs underway on PS853 at Woodvale on 7th March 1954. Both Phil Butler

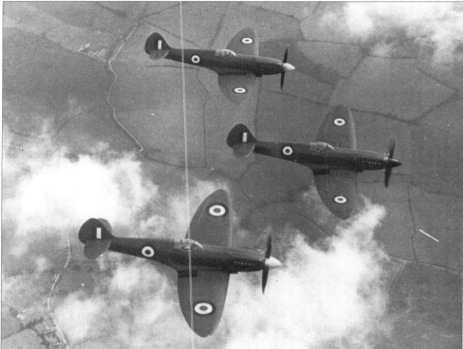

LF363 on the ground, and were welcomed by Air Marshal Sir Thomas Pike KCB CBE DFC*, the Air Officer Commanding-in-Chief, Fighter Command, who officially announced the formation of the Battle of Britain Flight, although in the early days it was more normally known as the Historic Aircraft Flight, and the aircraft were placed on the charge of the Station Flight at Biggin Hill.

For the bulk of their operational lives, the trio of Mk.XIX Spitfires had operated together on the THUM Flight at Woodvale, although each had seen a different variety of uses before taking up their meteorological duties. Of the three, PM631 perhaps saw the least use, spending most of its time following manufacture in November 1945 in storage, apart from a short period with 203 Advanced Flying School at Keevil, Wiltshire, from 6th May 1949 to 13th January 1950, before joining the THUM Flight at Hooton Park on 2nd July 1951.

Built by Vickers at Southampton, PS853 had a more interesting operational career, having been issued to the Central Photographic Reconnaissance Unit at Benson, Oxfordshire, on 13th January 1945. Thereafter, it passed to 16 Squadron at Melsbroek in Belgium, and later at Eindhoven in the Netherlands, before joining 268 Squadron at Celle in Germany. When 268 Squadron disbanded on 19th September 1945 it was renumbered 16 Squadron, and PS853 stayed with its old unit until moving to 29 MU at High Ercall, Shropshire, by 18th April 1946. After a period of storage in a number of MUs, PS853 was finally allotted to the THUM Flight on 16th April 1952.

The third of the Mk.XIX Spitfires, PS915, spent much of its career at Benson, serving there from 26th April 1945 with a number of units including 541 Squadron, 1 Pilot's Pool and the Photographic Reconnaissance Development Unit. On 8th July 1948 PS915 was allocated to 2 Squadron at Wunstorf in Germany, where it suffered a number of minor accidents, until allocated to the THUM Flight after repair on 4th June 1954.

PS853 at Woodvale in less happy circumstances, having overshot on landing following an attempt to depart for Duxford on 12th June 1957. Ken Ellis collection

On 11th July 1957, the three ex-THUM Flight Mk.XIX Spitfires were flown from Duxford to Biggin Hill. Peter Green collection

Hardly had the Flight formed when changes to its complement of aircraft began to occur. Unlike its two companions, PS915 was almost immediately retired from flying, and on 8th August it was flown to West Malling by Peter Thompson, now promoted to Group Captain, to take up display duties at first as 7548M, but this was changed to 7711M on 10th December. The departure of PS915 was made in exchange for another Spitfire, Mk.XVIE TE330, which was at West Malling, Kent, having earlier appeared at the Royal Tournament in July 1957, together with SL574 and TE476. TE330 had been refurbished at St Athan, Glamorgan, before being displayed at Earls Court, and was allocated to West Malling for ground instructional duties as 7449M. During August TE330 was transferred to Biggin Hill by road and was quickly made airworthy again, the instructional serial number being cancelled on 12th September. At Biggin Hill TE330 was placed on the charge of the 11 Group Communications Flight, and it did not transfer to the charge of the Station Flight with the remainder of the historic aircraft until March 1958. The further two Mk.XVI Spitfires that had also been displayed at the 1957 Royal Tournament, SL574 and TE476, were also obtained by Biggin Hill, and were officially transferred to the charge of the Station Flight on 20th February 1958.

On arrival at Biggin Hill, the three Spitfires were to join LF363, which by that time had received a camouflage colour scheme.
Francis K Mason

TE330 was one of the Mk.XIV Spitfires to succeed the Mk.XIXs and is seen here near Biggin Hill in 1958. Neville Franklin collection

During its active service life, SL574 was operated by the Empire Air Armament School at Manby, where it was photographed in 1947. via Andy Thomas

Of the Mk.XVI Spitfires, SL574 was built at Castle Bromwich and delivered to 6 MU at Brize Norton, Oxfordshire, on 14th August 1945, for storage. Its period of storage lasted until 30th September 1947, when it was issued to the Empire Air Armament School (EAAS) at Manby, Lincolnshire, where it suffered a minor flying accident on 28th October 1948.

TE476 taxies past a USAF Boeing KB-50J Superfortress at Bentwaters on 16th May 1959. C F E Smedley

TE476 and LF363 mingle with the aircraft of the 11 Group Communications Flight at North Weald in 1958.
Peter Green collection

After repair, SL574 rejoined the EAAS fleet until 19th July 1949, when it was transferred to the Central Gunnery School at Leconfield, Yorkshire, moving on 22nd November to 29 MU High Ercall for storage. On 16th April 1951 SL574 was taken on charge by 102 Flying Refresher School at North Luffenham, Rutland, where it remained until 12th October when it was returned to storage at 33 MU, Lyneham, Wiltshire, before being allocated to 3 Civilian Anti-Aircraft Co-operation Unit (CAACU) at Exeter on 15th October 1953. The aircraft made a brief debut in the film *Reach for the Sky* in August 1955 and remained at 3 CAACU until 25th June 1956, when it was transferred to 5 MU, Kemble, and declared non-effective stock on 16th August, until selected to appear at the Royal Tournament in 1957.

Completed in May 1945, TE330 spent its early life in storage before being allocated to 601 (County of London) Squadron Royal Auxiliary Air Force, based at Hendon, Middlesex. After a period of storage from March 1950, TE330 then went to 2 CAACU at Langham, Norfolk, in January 1954, before returning to store in April 1955. Transferred to non-effective stock on 16th July 1956 at Kemble, in January 1957 TE330 went to 32 MU, St Athan to be prepared for its appearance at the Royal Tournament.

The third Spitfire Mk.XVI to see service with the BBMF's precursors, TE476, was built at Castle Bromwich and flown to 39 MU at Colerne, Wiltshire, on 30th June 1945 for storage. Later transferred to 33 MU, Lyneham, it was not until 4th July 1951 that TE476 was issued to an active unit, 1 CAACU at Hornchurch, Essex, where it served until 11th September 1956, when it was retired to 5 MU, Kemble. Declared a non-effective airframe on 17th January 1957, TE476 was next moved to 32 MU, St Athan, where it was prepared for display at the 1957 Royal Tournament that July, having been allocated the instructional aircraft serial number 7451M. Unfortunately, the year 1958 was to see substantial reductions in the front line of the

The firecrew douse TE476 with foam following its wheels-up landing at Martlesham Heath on 10th September 1959.
Peter Green collection

The engine of SL574 comes under close scrutiny during recovery from the cricket ground at Bromley where it made a forced landing on 20th September 1959.
Neville Franklin collection

RAF as the effects of the 1957 Defence White Paper of Duncan Sandys took hold, and it was decided that Biggin Hill was to close to flying. As a result, on 28th February, the Battle of Britain Flight moved to North Weald, Essex, with one Hurricane (LF363), and a Spitfire contingent of three Mk.XVIs (TE330, TE476 and SL574) and two Mk.XIXs (PM631 and PS853) on charge.

Relocation and Reduction

No sooner had the Flight arrived at North Weald than there were moves to remove some of its aircraft, which saw Mk.XIX PS853 allocated to West Raynham, Norfolk, on 14th May 1958, for ground instructional duties. Surprisingly, the aircraft was struck off charge on 1st May for reduction to spares, although it was placed on display in

front of the station headquarters, having been allocated the instructional serial number 7548M formerly reserved for PS915.

A further reduction in the Flight's complement of airworthy aircraft came as moves were made to donate a Spitfire from the RAF to the United States Air Force Academy at Colorado Springs. One of the Mk.XVI Spitfires, TE330, was the aircraft selected to go and it was flown from North Weald to Odiham on 14th May 1958, where it was handed over in a ceremony held on 2nd July. The event was marked by flypasts from the Hurricane and a Spitfire of the Battle of Britain Flight, plus Javelins and Hunters, which were followed by an aerobatic display by 111 Squadron. Thereafter, TE330 was dismantled and loaded on a Douglas C-124 Globemaster II of the USAF for the flight to the USA. Today, TE330 can be seen in the USAF Museum at Wright-Patterson AFB, Ohio.

Fate was still working against the Battle of Britain Flight, however, for in the spring of 1958 it was decided that North Weald was also to close, so on 16th May it moved once again, this time to Martlesham Heath, Suffolk. Up to 1959, the Flight had operated its aircraft without trouble, but the events of that year were to be far different. The first of these occurred on 28th May, when SL574 made a wheels-up landing at Martlesham,

Further scrutiny of SL574's engine at Bromley. Note the inscription on the tool box lid by the port mainwheel, which reads 'Cpl Eardley R, Eng Fitter, BBMF'. This indicates that the title BBMF was in use as early as 1959, rather than being introduced during 1973 which is the accepted wisdom.
Peter Green collection

After the ignominy of Bromley, SL574 was relegated to static display duties at Bentley Priory, the HQ Fighter Command.
Neville Franklin collection

By the time the Flight moved to Norfolk it had reduced in strength to just two aircraft, LF363 and PM631, seen here in formation in September 1960, a year before the move took place. Robert Rudhall collection

Whilst at Binbrook PS853 proved a popular attraction, and is seen here being filmed by a BBC TV crew for the programme 'Look North'. Author's collection

but after repair by a party from 71 MU at Bicester, Oxfordshire, it was flying again by the end of July. A second wheels-up landing at Martlesham occurred on 10th September when Mk.XVI TE476 made a belly landing on the runway after the pilot forgot to lower the undercarriage prior to landing having returned shortly after take off with a failed radio. The pilot, Group Captain W A Theed, was uninjured.

More seriously, on the 20th September the Flight's other Mk.XVI, SL574, was taking part in the annual Battle of Britain flypast over London in company with Hurricane LF363 when it suffered an engine failure overhead Bromley, Kent. The pilot, Air Vice-Marshal H J Maguire, was able to execute a safe wheels-up landing on the cricket pitch of the OXO sports ground. However, despite extensive testing by Rolls-Royce, it was not possible to discover why the engine had failed, and this led to some far-reaching implications. Because the Spitfire Mk.XVI was powered by the Packard-built Merlin 266, it was decided that this variant of the Merlin was unsafe for further flight and the two aircraft were grounded. Of greater significance, further participation by the single-engined Hurricane and Spitfire in the City of London flypast was discontinued, and it was not until 1986 that Londoners would again hear the sound of a Spitfire over the capital.

With its usefulness to the Flight at an end, after being repaired SL574 was allocated for gate guardian duties at the Headquarters of Fighter Command at Bentley Priory, Middlesex, on 23rd November 1961.

PS853 and PM631 together at Binbrook in early 1964, where both aircraft had been involved in trials with the Lightnings of the Air Fighting Development Squadron and the Javelins of the resident 64 Squadron. Author's collection

Seen at Yeadon in 1959, AB910 carried the codes 'QJ-J' of 92 Squadron for many years, at first painted in narrow style. MAP

Britain Flight found itself on a front-line operational station within Fighter Command and its fortunes began to improve from there on.

Consolidation at Coltishall

Coltishall's Station Commander at the time, Group Captain R L Topp AFC, former leader of the 111 Squadron Aerobatic Team, 'The Black Arrows', quickly recognised the plight of the Flight and began the long task of gaining official recognition for its work and improving its professionalism and standards. He established minimum qualifications and training requirements for new pilots, who were generally drawn from the flight simulator section of Coltishall's resident 226 Operational Conversion Unit (OCU), which was equipped with the English Electric Lightning. With the support of Group Captain Topp, it was possible to arrange for pilot training on 'taildragger' aircraft and to ensure that time was made available for continuation training and display flying in each aircraft type, whilst parallel arrangements were made to support the engineering activities.

The first boost to the Flight came in April 1964, with the return of Spitfire Mk.XIX PS853, which had left the flight at North Weald in 1958 for the Central Fighter Establishment (CFE) at West Raynham. After a spell as a gate guardian, PS853 was restored to airworthy condition and was officially taken on charge by the CFE Communications Flight on 31st October 1962.

A similar fate befell TE476, which was struck off charge on 6th January 1960, but was reallocated to Coltishall, Norfolk, as gate guardian on 31st January. Later the aircraft went to Neatishead, Norfolk, for use in a similar role. SL574 is now displayed at San Diego, California, and TE476 is part of American Kermit Weeks' collection.

Like all of the Flight's former bases, Martlesham Heath too began to run down, and on 3rd November 1961, the Battle of Britain Flight was moved again, to Horsham St Faith, near Norwich, with its meagre fleet of the faithful Hurricane LF363, and Spitfire

Mk.XIX PM631. On arriving at Horsham, the historic aircraft were serviced by the personnel of the 12 Group Communications Flight, which carried the Hurricane and the Spitfire as an unrecognised addition to their normal duties. However, like every other station that had housed the Battle of Britain Flight in the turbulent first five years of its life, Horsham was also scheduled to close, to become the civil airport for Norwich. Fortunately, there was then a general realisation of the worth of the Flight, and on 1st April 1963 the two aircraft were moved to Coltishall. For the first time the Battle of

Whilst with the CFE, PS853 was involved in a number of trials including an assessment of the use of high performance jet fighters like the Lightning against piston-engined opposition, such as was being encountered by the USAF in South East Asia. The aircraft then moved to Binbrook, Lincolnshire, with the CFE in October 1962, where it continued its trials work with the Lightnings and Hunters of its parent unit, although during a period of unserviceability it was joined by the Flight's PM631. However, PS853 was allocated to the Battle of Britain Flight on 14th April 1964, in time to participate in some of the 50 displays that the Flight gave throughout the country that year.

A fourth Spitfire joined the Flight at the end of the 1965 display season in the shape of Mk.VB AB910, which had been owned firstly by Group Captain, later Air Commodore, Allen H Wheeler, during which time it carried the civil registration G-AISU, before being sold to Vickers Armstrong Ltd in 1955. The aircraft was flown in to Coltishall on 16th September by Jeffrey Quill, the company's Chief Test Pilot for so many years and inextricably linked with much of the development test flying of the Spitfire. AB910 was readily absorbed into the Flight, continuing to wear the squadron markings and code letters 'QJ-J' of 92 Squadron applied by Vickers. With three Spitfires (AB910, PM631 and PS853) and its faithful Hurricane (LF363), the Flight settled down to a period of stability.

As the spare parts supply for the aircraft gradually dwindled away, the number of displays that could be flown was forced to be reduced until in 1965 just 20 were carried out, with even less attended in 1966. This trend was probably the boost needed to ensure that the ground support arrangements were properly established and that a more professional approach was taken to the spares support for the aircraft.

The Battle of Britain Film

The year 1968 was to be something of a milestone in the life of the Battle of Britain Flight, for it was during that year that some two or three years of effort by Spitfire Productions Ltd came to fruition with the making of the film, *The Battle of Britain*. As a result of the efforts of the film's principal technical advisor, Group Captain 'Hamish' Mahaddie, the Ministry of Defence approved the use of the Flight's aircraft for the flying sequences, together with a number of former gate guardian aircraft for static scenes. Technical facilities were made available at Henlow, Bedfordshire, and filming began in Spain in March 1968. From May 1968 filming switched to England, where it was centred on Duxford, although the unkind summer weather resulted in many of the aircraft, including those of the Battle of Britain Flight, being sent to Montpellier in Southern France to carry out some of the filming in the clear skies of the Mediterranean. Eventually, the job was done, and by the end of September the aerial sequences were complete, although throughout the summer the Flight had met its usual display commitment in addition to the rigorous filming schedule. For the whole of the period of filming the RAF's aircraft were flown by RAF pilots, who were supported by some of the groundcrew from Coltishall.

The Battle of Britain Flight made a substantial contribution to the film's available fleet of airworthy aircraft, all of its aircraft being used in one way or another. Indeed, such was the Flight's commitment to the film that its three Spitfires flew a total of 268 hours during the year, rather than the planned display flying task of just 100 hours. With the premiere of the film planned for 15th September 1969, the Spitfire task of the Flight was increased to 130 hours for the year in anticipation of the increased profile caused by the expected release of the film.

While engaged in making the film *The Battle of Britain*, the normal programme of displays continued throughout 1968. LF363 is seen at the Leuchars Battle of Britain display in September 1968.
Neville Franklin collection

More significantly, the film was probably a turning point, not only for the Flight, but also for the whole of the British aircraft preservation movement which suddenly realised that wartime fighters, especially the Spitfire, could be maintained in an airworthy condition and flown regularly as a potential air display attraction.

Spitfire Mk.IIA P7350

The added significance of the film for the Flight was that it gained a fourth airworthy Spitfire, in the guise of Mk.IIA P7350. Built at Castle Bromwich, P7350 was taken on charge by the RAF at 6 MU, Brize Norton, in August 1940 and from 16th September it operated with 266 Squadron at Hornchurch, Wittering, Northamptonshire, and later with 603 (City of Edinburgh) Squadron at North Weald, thereby seeing operational service in the Battle of Britain. Surviving the war, P7350 was declared surplus to require-

ments in 1948 and was sold for scrap to John Dale Ltd, of London Colney, Hertfordshire, which donated the aircraft to the museum at RAF Colerne for static display. Coded in former 266 Squadron codes 'ZH-' (although of the Typhoon era), P7350 was displayed at Colerne for many years until 1967, when it was found to be in such excellent condition that it was taken to Henlow to be restored to airworthy standard and registered as G-AWIJ for use in the film *The Battle of Britain*. It remained owned by the RAF throughout, despite the civilian identity.

With the end of the filming, P7350 was taken on charge by the Battle of Britain Flight on 5th November 1968, and flown to Coltishall where it was readied for a new life of display flying. Because of the general condition it was in after the filming, the so-called 'Baby' Spitfire was sent to 5 MU at Kemble for respray on 28th April 1969, returning to Coltishall on 12th June once again restored to the 'ZH-' markings of 266 Squadron. The correct code used by the squadron at the time of the Battle of Britain was 'UO-'.

Although the Flight's aircraft involved in the filming were flown throughout by RAF pilots, there was some controversy at the end of the filming that the aircraft had been allowed to deteriorate to an unacceptable standard, and as a result it was agreed that the other aircraft would also go to 5 MU for stripping, cleaning and respraying in camouflage colours but using polyurethane paint. Engines were also something of a problem for the Flight, and on 30th January 1969, Boulton Paul Sea Balliol WL732 was

Below left: **AB910 is seen here in the wartime codes of 145 Squadron, the shadow squadron number allocated to 226 OCU which provided pilots for the Flight's aircraft.** Neville Franklin collection

Below right: **When it first reappeared following the Battle of Britain film, LF363 carried its squadron markings painted in thin strokes, as seen here at Wethersfield on 24th May 1969.** Author

Bottom: **PZ865 was rolled out at Langley in July 1944 in company with Hawker's surviving Hart, G-ABMR.** Francis K Mason

flown into Coltishall from Boscombe Down, Wilts, for its airworthy engine to be removed and fitted to Spitfire AB910, which was sent for repainting at Kemble on 6th March, returning to Coltishall on 28th April. Unfortunately, the intended new squadron codes to depict 145 Squadron which were painted on AB910 at Kemble were wrongly applied as 'PB-T', rather than the correct 'SO-T', but this was quickly corrected after the aircraft's return.

The condition of LF363 was somewhat worse than that of the Spitfires, and it was flown from Coltishall to 27 MU at Shawbury, Shropshire, on 6th March 1969, to have its fabric replaced. It was then flown to Kem-

ble for painting on 14th April, before returning to Coltishall on 28th April. Thus, by the peak of the 1969 flying display season, the Battle of Britain Flight had received an additional Spitfire in the shape of a genuine veteran of the Battle, all of its aircraft had been repainted and the Hurricane's fabric had been renewed. At the same time there was also a hint of further expansion, and the Flight managed to obtain Fieseler Fi 156C-7 Storch VP546 (formerly Luftwaffe werke nummer 475081 and evaluated in Britain as Air Ministry No 101) with a view to making it airworthy, although this project was discouraged because it was diverting scarce manpower from the Flight's own aircraft.

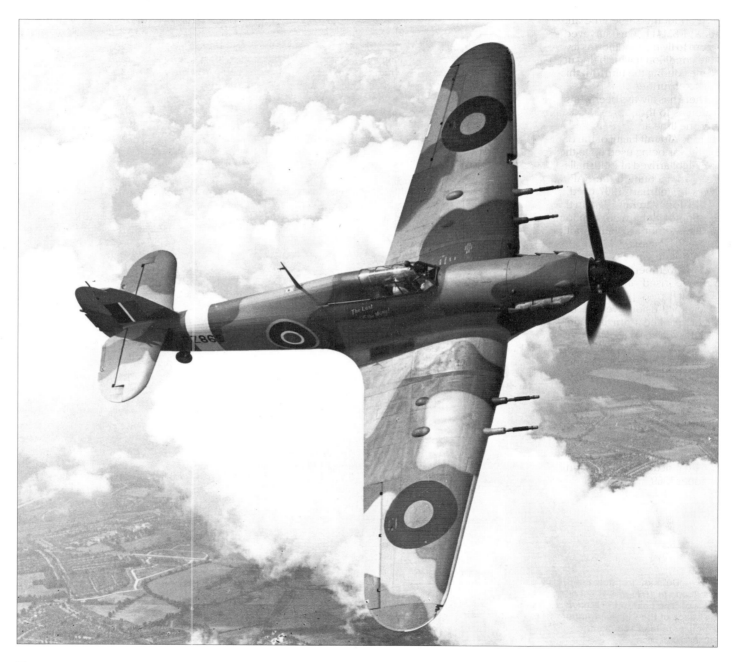

At about the same time another Spitfire, Mk.XVI SM411, was surveyed for possible return to flying condition as it was in reasonable condition having being used in taxiing scenes during the film, but this project was not taken further.

There has always been considerable confusion as to the proper title of the Flight at any one time and in most accounts, the title Historic Aircraft Flight or the Battle of Britain Flight was being used up to the point when the Flight arrived at Coltishall in 1963. However, an account in the RAF magazine *Air Clues* in February 1967 used the terminology Historic Aircraft Flight in the text, whilst the photographs were captioned Battle of Britain Memorial Flight. Another *Air Clues* article in November 1969 used the title Battle of Britain Flight, whilst in a letter dated 2nd November 1968, the Ministry of Defence used the term RAF Memorial Flight. It is most probable that this seeming official confusion over the true title of the Flight resulted from its 'unofficial' status, and this was not resolved formally until the manpower was properly established and accounted for, which seemed to occur at Coltishall in about 1968. Indeed, the Battle of Britain Memorial Flight was formally promulgated as being located at RAF Coltishall with effect from 1st June 1969, by organisation memorandum 93/69 which was published in Secret Document 155 (SD155). The Flight first appeared in the next edition of SD161, Locations of RAF Units, dated 1st October 1969.

George Bulman first flew the prototype Hurricane in 1935 and is seen here at the helm of 'The Last of the Many!' Note the presence of the four wing-mounted cannon, which were later removed.
Author's collection

Hurricane Mk.IIC PZ865

It was not long, however, before further expansion came with the arrival in March 1972 of the Flight's second Hurricane Mk.IIC, PZ865, which had been completed at Hawker's Langley factory on 27th July 1944, the last of more than 14,000 Hurricanes to be built. The aircraft was named 'The Last of the Many!', and this name was painted on the fuselage sides, just aft of the cockpit. PZ865 was rolled out in the presence of Hawker's remaining Hart, G-ABMR, bedecked in banners to proclaim the service history of the Hurricane family. PZ865 then made its first flight in the hands of George Bulman, the man who had flown the prototype Hurricane on its first flight on the 6th November 1935.

With the end of the war, PZ865 was acquired by Hawkers and on 1st May 1950 registered G-AMAU. After civilianisation, which entailed the removal of its weapons and painting in a civil colour scheme of Royal blue and gold, the colours of HRH The Princess Margaret, G-AMAU took part in a number of air races during the early 1950s, including the King's Cup, during which it was often flown by Group Captain Peter Townsend. PZ865 also appeared in a number of films, including *Angels One-Five*, where it carried the code letters 'US-B' and the serial number P2619 to depict an aircraft of 56 Squadron. Following further use as a company communications aircraft, Hawkers decided in 1960 to refurbish PZ865 and when it reappeared it was resplendent in its military colours again, carrying both its military serial number plus its civil registration, the latter being applied in small letters on the fuselage side underneath the tailplane.

Thereafter, PZ865 continued in use at Dunsfold, where it found a key role as a chase plane for the trials of the Sea Fury T.20S target tugs destined for Germany. It was also found to be an ideal vehicle from which to monitor critical phases of the flight trials of the P.1127 'jump-jet' prototype, especially the transition between wing-borne flight and jet-borne lift, where the Hurricane's low speed envelope was found to be ideal. A further film appearance was made in *The Battle of Britain* in 1968, whereupon PZ865 was refurbished again, including replacement of its fabric covering. A period of static display followed as part of the Hawker Museum, until it was restored to flying condition in 1971, and on 30th March 1972 PZ865 was presented to the BBMF at Coltishall. With the arrival of a new Hurricane it transpired that there was an intention to then transfer LF363 to the RAF Museum for static display at Hendon, and it was duly allotted there on 5th April 1972. However, this suggestion caused a furore, and the allotment was quickly cancelled on 11th May, with both Hurricanes being retained in flying condition to the delight of the public.

Lancaster B.I PA474

Having absorbed a second Hurricane, the Flight was soon destined to receive its largest, if most controversial, new arrival in the shape of the RAF's sole airworthy Lancaster bomber, PA474. The Lancaster had been built by Vickers Armstrong at its Chester factory as a B Mk.I, which was modified to Far East standards for use on 'Tiger Force', the British element of the final assault on Japan. By the time of its first flight in August 1945, however, the war with Japan had ended abruptly and PA474 was delivered to 38 MU, Llandow, Glamorgan, where it was placed into storage having flown less than four hours.

A series of modifications carried out at Baginton (Armstrong Whitworth's plant at what is now Coventry Airport) saw PA474 converted to PR Mk.1 standard to permit it to carry two reconnaissance cameras and an operator, whilst to protect the crew from the blistering heat of the African sun, where it was destined to operate, many of the perspex panels in the rear of the cockpit canopy were removed and replaced with metal items.

In racing trim, PZ865 was painted in a striking blue and white colour scheme with a gold-coloured spinner. Francis K Mason

After refurbishment and being returned to military markings, PZ865 was used as a chase-plane for P.1127 development trials. Ken Ellis collection

After a further period of storage, PA474 was finally allocated to an operational unit and was delivered to Benson to join 82 Squadron on 27th November 1948. At that time the squadron was operating from Takoradi in West Africa, and PA474 was sent to assist with the task of carrying out a photographic survey as a prelude to the production of new maps of the area.

PA474 returned to Benson on 22nd July 1949, moving on to Avro's factory at Woodford, south of Manchester, for major servicing in April 1950, before returning to 82 Squadron, which by then was operating from Eastleigh, in Kenya. Following its return to Benson again on 18th February 1952, the Lancaster left 82 Squadron and from 26th May was loaned to Flight Refuelling Ltd at Tarrant Rushton, Dorset, for conversion to a pilotless drone. A major servicing was carried out at Tarrant Rushton, but the drone conversion programme was suspended and on 7th March 1954, PA474 was flown to the College of Aeronautics at Cranfield, Bedfordshire, to serve as a flight-trials platform.

At Cranfield, PA474 was intended to conduct research into the boundary layer airflow over a wing surface, which entailed fitting a series of wing sections and other apparatus onto the top of the fuselage. The first wing section was installed between 10th and 30th April 1956, and PA474 first flew in this configuration on 4th May. From 25th October 1958, a section of Folland Midge lightweight jet fighter wing was installed, the aircraft making its first flight for these trials on 27th February 1959. This installation gave way in September 1962 to the Handley Page laminar flow wing, which also required the installation of two 60hp Budworth gas turbine engines in the rear fuselage which were required to suck air from the boundary layer of the experimental wing.

Throughout its trials work at Cranfield, PA474 flew little more than 100 hours, and when its engines became life expired it was

decided to replace the aircraft with Avro Lincoln B.2 RF342. All of the special equipment fitted to PA474 was removed and transferred to RF342 and, on 22nd April 1964, PA474 was flown to Wroughton where it was to be serviced by 15 MU on behalf of the Air Historical Branch, to whom it had been allocated pending formation of the RAF Museum. At 15 MU, PA474 was restored and painted in wartime colours, before being flown to Henlow on 25th September where the potential exhibits for the RAF Museum were being gathered. Unfortunately, the hangars at Henlow were too small to accommodate the Lancaster and its stablemate Lincoln B.2 RF398, and both aircraft had to sit out in the open.

Even after its arrival at Cranfield for trials flying, PA474 remained in the colours of 82 Squadron. Paddy Porter collection

After a highly successful transit flight from Henlow, PA474 taxies to a halt at Waddington on 18th August 1965. Neville Franklin collection

Knowing the plight of PA474, and knowing that the RAF Museum was unlikely to materialise for some years, the Commanding Officer of 44 Squadron at Waddington, Lincolnshire, was able to persuade the Air Historical Branch to release PA474 to be flown back to Waddington where it could

The Lancaster made its first flight after restoration on 7th November 1967. With front and rear turrets fitted, but without guns, the aircraft is seen overflying Waddington during that flight.
Author's collection

Opposite page: In preparation for the ceremonies to mark the formation of Strike Command, one of the first formation rehearsals was carried out on 5th March 1968. On that day PA474, accompanied by LF363 and AB910, toured a number of airfields including the RAF College at Cranwell, seen here.
Rolls-Royce via Francis K Mason

be placed under cover and perhaps restored. After a series of functional and other maintenance checks, the flight to Waddington was made on 18th August 1965, whereupon restoration began. The aircraft was painted in 44 Squadron markings, code letters 'KM-B', to represent the aircraft flown by Squadron John Nettleton who led the raid by 44 and 97 Squadrons against the U-boat engine factory at Augsburg on 17th April 1942. Nettleton's aircraft was the only 44 Squadron machine to return from the raid, and he was awarded the Victoria Cross for outstanding leadership.

After a great deal of spare time effort by the groundcrew on 44 Squadron, the AHB finally agreed that the aircraft could be flown for the purpose of making an air test, which was carried out on 7th November 1967. The crew on this occasion was Waddington's Station Commander, Group Captain Arthur Griffiths AFC, who had flown Lancasters until 1949, Squadron Leader Ken Hayward, of the 1 Group Standardisation Flight, who had 800 hours of Lancaster flying, and Chief Technician Ken Terry, who was a Lancaster Flight Engineer during the

war, and who had overseen much of the restoration work on the aircraft. The successful flight lasted for 17 minutes, and authority was granted for the aircraft to make a limited number of displays over the next year.

By early 1968, display rehearsals were in full swing, and on 5th March PA474 made a formation flight in company with Hurricane LF363 and Spitfire AB910 of the BBMF as a prelude to the Stand-down of Bomber and Fighter Commands on the formation of Strike Command on 30th April. Once again flown by Group Captain Griffiths, PA474 took part in the Bomber Command Stand-down ceremony at Scampton, but its first major public display was at Abingdon, on 14th and 15th June, at the Royal Review of the RAF on the occasion of its 50th anniversary. By the time its authority to fly expired on 30th October 1968, PA474 had given some 15 displays and flown about 40 hours during the year.

As the winter progressed, thoughts began to turn to the 1969 season, and a request was received for the Lancaster to fly over the D-Day beaches on 6th June, 1969, the

25th anniversary of the landings. After a series of high-level representations, authority was granted for a second year of display flying under the same conditions as had been imposed for 1968. Broadly, Waddington had to support the aircraft from within its own resources, a requirement which placed a heavy burden on the station, and as the Lancaster's popularity boomed Waddington found it harder and harder to support the aircraft properly and give it the tender loving care that was undoubtedly needed.

A solution had to be found, and a decision was taken to transfer PA474 to the BBMF at Coltishall, where expertise on its Merlin engines and spare parts were more readily available. The transfer took place on 20th November 1973, amidst a crescendo of protest from the people of Lincolnshire, to whom the Lancaster had such strong emotional ties. In an attempt to stop the transfer, the Lincolnshire Lancaster Appeal Committee was formed, and a petition of 20,000 signatures was presented to the Ministry of Defence, seeking return of the aircraft to Lincolnshire. In a gesture perhaps aimed more at appeasing the people of Lincolnshire, the Ministry of Defence did allow PA474 to be officially adopted by the City of Lincoln, and the City's name and Coat of

PA474 dips in salute at Bentley Priory during the Fighter Command stand-down ceremony on 30th April 1968, the day that Strike Command was formed. Author's collection

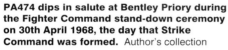

By August 1971 guns had been fitted to the front and rear turrets, although the propeller tips were painted in quite non-authentic red and white stripes. Bruce Robertson

Arms were applied to the left hand side of the aircraft, just forward of the cockpit in May 1974. The official adoption was celebrated at Waddington on 8th May 1975 with a parade of the Standards of the four resident Vulcan squadrons in front of the Lancaster, with the Mayor of Lincoln in attendance.

Move to Coningsby

Proudly wearing its 'City of Lincoln' title, the Lancaster visited Coningsby on 18th July 1974, for compatibility trials with the station's variety of hangars as planning went ahead to relocate the BBMF as part of a reorganisation of the RAF's bases following the introduction to service of the Anglo-French SEPECAT Jaguar strike aircraft. On 18th June 1975, executive authority for the Flight to move to Coningsby was given, and its authorised flying task for 1976 was increased to 240 hours for the fighters to allow for the move, whereupon the task was to revert to 200 hours per year; the Lancaster was granted 55 flying hours, and the de Havilland Canada Chipmunk T.10 (see page 27) a total of 300. It was therefore after an absence of almost two and a half years that PA474 was to return to its adopted county, on 1st March 1976, in company with three of the BBMF's Spitfires and one of the Hurricanes, whilst Spitfire AB910 and Hurricane PZ865 followed a few days later. Also travelling to Coningsby was the hulk of Spitfire Mk.IX MK732, which had been used at Coltishall as a source of spare parts.

Immediately after the BBMF arrived at Coningsby, PA474 took part in the French film *Lieutenant Karl*, after which work began on installing a mid-upper turret. Such was the importance attached to the aircraft of the BBMF in the eyes of the public that the code letters and markings they carried became something of a celebrity matter. Indeed, the subject became so prominent that on 13th July 1977, the Under Secretary of State for the RAF agreed that the codes and markings carried by the aircraft could be changed at appropriate intervals. It was therefore decided in October 1977 to next commemorate the first squadrons to receive the Hurricane and the Spitfire by applying the markings of 111 and 19 Squadrons respectively.

In keeping with normal practice, the Lancaster underwent winter servicing every year, which always included a thorough inspection for corrosion. It was during such an inspection in the winter of 1977-78 that severe corrosion was found in rivets exposed to the engine exhaust efflux, including those in the engine nacelles, the flaps and the wing lower skin. This entailed such extensive repairs that the aircraft did

The City of Lincoln formally adopted PA474 at a ceremony at Waddington held on 8th May 1975. Bruce Robertson

not fly at all during 1978. Returned to flying status in April 1979, PA474 was repainted in 617 Squadron markings at Lyneham during September, but throughout the following winter and over the next few years a steady programme of structural inspection and repair was carried out to ensure the continued integrity of the aircraft.

Whilst the Lancaster was grounded, the BBMF suffered another tragedy which resulted in the near destruction of one of its Spitfires, but fortunately without injury to its pilot. On 21st August 1978, AB910 was preparing to depart from the International Air Show at Bex in Switzerland, and had just begun its take-off run, when a Dutch North American Harvard turned onto the runway in front of the Spitfire. The aircraft collided but there was no fire, although AB910 was substantially damaged.

Support Aircraft and Activities

Whilst the spotlight always tends to shine on the principal aircraft, the BBMF also operates a small number of support aircraft which are essential to the safe delivery of the annual display programme. Smallest but perhaps most significant of these is the humble Chipmunk, the Flight having operated a number over the years, including WP855 and its current mount WK518, now painted in the colours of the RAF College, Cranwell and a worthy display subject in its own right. The Chipmunk serves many functions, but it is principally used for pilot training and checking out new pilots in the techniques of 'taildragging', in addition to use by the 'old boys' for keeping their hand in after the usual routine of flying Panavia Tornado F Mk.3s from Coningsby's resident 56 (Reserve) Squadron. The Chipmunk is also used as an aerial reconnaissance mount to carry out airborne checks of new display locations before they are flown with one of the fighters or the Lancaster.

Serving a much wider role is the BBMF's de Havilland Devon C.2/2, VP981, which was previously used by 207 Squadron as a

communications aircraft at Northolt, Greater London, until the end of June 1984. Whilst operational, 207 Squadron rendered valuable help to the BBMF, providing logistic support and a fully equipped escort aircraft when the Flight was deployed away from Coningsby, at first using Beagle Basset CC.1s and later Devons. The escort role was an import safety issue, because of the limited radio and avionics fit of the fighters, with the additional crew and capability of the Devon coming into its own during transits through controlled airspace, over water and on flights overseas. The need for the Devon was well illustrated by the 1984 season, which included 122 events attended by one or more aircraft, of which two were overseas.

There was a further training role for the Devon, which began to take on more prominence as the demise of the Avro Shackleton AEW.2 grew closer. Until then, the Lancaster captains were authorised for five hours pre-season flying on the Shackleton, although the co-pilots were not, and it was necessary to find a suitable aircraft to take its place.

Having been grounded throughout the 1978 season for structural repairs, after the 1979 season the Lancaster was painted in the colours of 617 Squadron. MAP

Having evaluated the Hawker Siddeley HS.125 communications jet, HS Andover transport and the Scottish Aviation Jetstream light transport, the Devon was found to be the most suitable aircraft. During the 1984 season, the BBMF received *ad hoc* support from the Finningley Jetstreams, and it was not until 30th April 1985 that authority was granted for Devon C.2/2 VP981 to be allocated to the BBMF. VP981 is an historic aircraft in its own right, having been first handed over to the RAF on 3rd January 1949. After two display seasons with the BBMF, VP981 went to Kemble for Minor 'Star' servicing between 26th September and 5th December 1986, whilst it went to Rolls-Royce at Filton for major servicing over the winter of 1991-92.

An aircraft with a little-known connection with the BBMF is Hawker Sea Fury T Mk.20S, VZ345, which was one of 60 such advanced continuation trainers built for the Royal Navy and delivered between 1950 and 1952. In the case of VZ345, it was completed on 13th March 1950, and taken on charge by the RN on 27th April, at the Anthorn Receipt and Despatch Unit, Cumberland. After a period of storage, VZ345 was delivered to 1832 Squadron at Culham, Oxfordshire, on 14th June 1951, although it was later to spend a considerable period in storage. However, by 1957 Hawkers began to buy large numbers of Sea Furies from the RN for refurbishment and subsequent sale overseas and VZ345 was included in the package, being struck off charge on 11th July 1957.

Following refurbishment the aircraft was delivered to Bonn on 16th September 1958, as D-FATA of the Deutsche Luftfahrt Beratungdienst (DLB). D-FATA was at first used for continuation training, but in April 1959 it was fitted with Swedish-made target-towing gear which increased the all-up-weight of the aircraft and resulted in it being re-registered D-CATA. Based at Lübeck for maintenance, the aircraft was often operated out of Wiesbaden and Köln-Wahn on target towing duties in support of the Luftwaffe. Eventually, the German Sea Furies were declared surplus to requirements and were sold, having been replaced by Rockwell OV-10 Broncos. Subsequently, D-CATA was presented to the Aeroplane & Armament Experimental Establishment (A&AEE) at Boscombe Down by the A&AEE's German counterparts in Germany, Erprobungstelle 61 at Manching, and was flown from Wahn to Boscombe Down on 15th October 1974, where its previous serial number VZ345 was reallocated.

At Boscombe Down VZ345 was taken on as a restoration project by the civilian apprentices of the A&AEE, working under the supervision of their instructors. Over a period of some five years, the aircraft was restored to flying condition, and during 1979 it was agreed that it could be flown as a training aircraft for new pilots joining the BBMF before they moved on to fly the historic fighters. Officially on the charge of the BBMF, VZ345 remained at Boscombe Down until it was officially allotted to the MoD Procurement Executive air fleet based at Boscombe Down, on loan, on 2nd December 1980. However, after some five years of operations, on 17th April 1985, VZ345 overturned on landing at Boscombe Down, causing considerable damage to the fuselage, as a result of which it was made Category 5 (Scrap) on 13th May, having flown a total of 6,667 hours. After preliminary repair by the apprentices, VZ345 was found too badly damaged for restoration to flying condition and it was moved to Yeovilton on 24th November 1992, and subsequently in mid-1994 to British Aerospace at Brough, North Humberside, to assist in the restoration to flying condition of the Royal Navy's Sea Fury FB Mk.11 VR930.

Visitor Centre

Another function which has subsequently grown to become a key activity in support of the BBMF has been the Visitor Centre, which was opened at the BBMF's hangar at Coningsby in April 1986. In a joint initiative with Lincolnshire County Council and Lincolnshire's Lancaster Association, members of the public now have the opportunity to tour the Flight's hangar at Coningsby each day, with the exception of public holi-

days and weekends. In addition to the BBMF itself, there is a small museum of relevant displays and a souvenir shop, whilst expert guides are provided by volunteers drawn from the Lincolnshire's Lancaster Association. Clearly, there is no guarantee that all of the aircraft will be there at any given time as they may well be away from Coningsby undergoing maintenance or positioning for a display.

Visitors may, however, have the opportunity to see the aircraft being moved out of the hangar for engine runs, or to take off and give a practice display as the pilots work up for the coming season. Whilst the aircraft are in the hangar there might also be the opportunity to watch some of the maintenance work being carried out, or to see the groundcrew completing the many tasks that are essential to keep the aircraft clean and ready for flight. A tour of the BBMF's hangar and the Visitor Centre at Coningsby is almost the only opportunity available to the public today to see the RAF at close quarters as it goes about its day-to-day work, and the joint initiative of the local

authority, an association of enthusiasts and the Ministry of Defence must be applauded.

Further Acquisitions

As a result of the generosity of British Aerospace (BAe), the BBMF was to see the return of another of its founding aircraft, Spitfire Mk.XIX PS915, which had been restored to flying condition at Samlesbury, Lancashire. After being used at Coningsby between October 1977 and March 1980 for the trial installation of a Griffon Mk.58 engine from a Shackleton, PS915 was taken from Brawdy, Dyfed, to Samlesbury on 13th June 1984 for restoration to flying condition. After an extensive rebuild using modern materials where necessary, and having been rewired for 24-volt electrics and fitted with a Griffon Mk.58, PS915 took to the air again for the first time since 1957 at Samlesbury on 16th December 1986. The aircraft was then transferred to nearby Warton for a period of flying by the BAe test pilots before it was allotted to the BBMF on 20th March 1987, when its instructional aircraft number 7711M was cancelled.

The extent of the damage to AB910 caused during its accident at Bex is clearly visible as the aircraft undergoes repair at Abingdon.
Tim R Badham via Ken Ellis collection

Escort aircraft for the BBMF were first provided by the Bassets of 207 Squadron, as denoted by this formation en route from Coltishall in 1970. Paddy Porter collection

The BBMF eventually obtained its own Devon which was later painted in the Flight's own markings. MAP

Unfortunately, the planned delivery to Coningsby was delayed for a few weeks when PS915 suffered slight damage to the propeller when it tipped up during engine runs just after landing at Warton following a test flight on 4th February 1987. It was not officially handed over to the BBMF until 24th March.

Another unique aircraft to join the Flight was Douglas Dakota III ZA947, which was transferred from the Defence Research Agency (DRA) in 1993. This aircraft was built some 50 years earlier, in March 1942, at Long Beach, California, as a C-47A-60-DL Skytrain under contract for the USAAF, being allocated the serial number 42-24338. However, the Dakota did not see service with the USAAF, and was delivered direct to the Royal Canadian Air Force (RCAF), where it was taken on charge on 16th September 1943, with the serial number 661. Between October and December 1944, 661 served with 164 Squadron (RCAF) and was based at Manston, Kent, for part of that time. By the early 1950s it was reported flying with the RCAF's Central Experimental and Proving Establishment Detachment at Suffield, Alberta, later returning to Europe by May 1963 to serve with 109 Flight (RCAF) at Grostenquin, France, as part of the 1st Air Division of the RCAF in Europe. During this period, the Dakota was frequently seen in the UK, especially at Prestwick, Ayrshire, but on 12th August 1963, 109 Flight was disbanded and by 1969 661 was to be found in storage at Prestwick.

Having a need for an aircraft such as the Dakota for trials and communications duties, the then Royal Aircraft Establishment (RAE) bought 661 from Scottish Aviation, at which point some confusion arose over its true identity. The aircraft was given the serial number of an earlier RAF Dakota, KG661, which had been struck off charge following a flying accident on 13th December 1944. Having confused 661 with KG661, the aircraft was painted as such before it was delivered to the RAE at West Freugh,

near Dumfries, in May 1971 to begin an active life as part of the RAE's trials fleet, undertaking such tasks as dropping sonobuoys and acting as launch platform for remote-controlled vehicles.

Whilst at West Freugh, the aircraft was named 'Portpatrick Princess' but, in June 1978, it was transferred to the RAE Transport Flight at Farnborough, at which point doubts were raised about its true identity. The doubts were confirmed and once its true identity was revealed, the Dakota was allocated a totally new serial number, ZA947, in June 1979. Over the years, the Dakota had been a regular attender at air shows, both as 'KG661' and as ZA947, including the 40th anniversary celebrations of the Berlin Air Lift, which were held at Berlin/Tempelhof in May 1989. However, shortly after the Berlin celebrations, the aircraft suffered some damage at Farnborough when the port undercarriage leg collapsed during the pre-take off engine run-up checks, causing damage to the engine, propeller and wing. Taken to Coventry for repairs by Air Atlantique, ZA947 returned to Farnborough on 16th October, 1990.

Having celebrated the Dakota's 50th anniversary at Farnborough on 17th March

1992, the DRA saw no further use for the aircraft and it was declared surplus to requirements. Fortunately, the Colonel Commandant of the Parachute Regiment was aware of the Dakota's plight, and that it might be sold, and in October 1992 had written to the Chief of the Air Staff proposing that the aircraft be retained to participate in the various anniversary celebrations expected during 1994 and 1995.

Following detailed investigations, this was agreed, and in March 1993 approval was granted for ZA947 to join the BBMF. After major servicing with Air Atlantique's engineering division at Coventry, the Dakota was flown to Marham, Norfolk, in June 1993 where it was repainted in the colours of 271 Squadron to depict the individual aircraft flown by Flight Lieutenant David Lord, who received the posthumous award of the Victoria Cross following the Arnhem operation of September 1944.

On purchase by the RAE, KG661 was named 'Portpatrick Princess', which was inscribed on the blue cheatline below the cockpit. MAP

Having discovered the aircraft's true identity, the Dakota was allocated a new serial number ZA947 and was later painted in the RAE's distinctive red, white and blue colour scheme. MAP

Making the obligatory flypast over Lincoln, ZA947 was painted in wartime camouflage colours on joining the BBMF.
Author's collection

The Fight for LF363

The arrival of the Dakota went some way to offset what has perhaps been the Flight's most significant accident in its long if uncertain history. On the afternoon of 11th September 1991, Hurricane LF363 was in transit from Coningsby to Jersey in company with the Lancaster and a Spitfire to attend the Jersey Air Show when, approximately three miles north of Stamford, Lincolnshire, its engine suddenly hesitated but continued to run roughly. The pilot therefore decided to divert to the nearest airfield, Wittering, Cambridgeshire, to the immediate south.

It became clear to the pilot that the residual engine power was insufficient for the aircraft to maintain height. Having crossed the eastern airfield boundary and with the aircraft in a right turn at only 100 ft above the ground, the engine cut completely. Finding the path straight ahead obstructed, the pilot continued the turn in an attempt to reach the runway, but the Hurricane's right wing touched the ground and the aircraft cartwheeled.

LF363 came to rest in an upright attitude on the end of the runway, but fire subsequently spread from the base of the cockpit and engulfed the pilot. Despite having suffered a broken ankle in the impact and having difficulty releasing his parachute harness, the pilot was able to evacuate the aircraft although he sustained severe burns to his legs. Unfortunately, despite the immediate attendance of the Wittering fire crews was unable to prevent the fire from consuming almost the whole of the aircraft, which was recovered to Coningsby for a technical inquiry into the reason for the engine failure.

Following extensive investigation it was established that the engine had begun to run roughly and eventually failed because of a broken camshaft on one of its banks of cylinders. The complete loss of power had occurred when the aircraft was in a position from which a successful forced landing could not be achieved.

The humble Chipmunk plays a vital role in the BBMF's operations. WP855 is seen here undergoing maintenance at Coningsby in February 1983. **Paddy Porter collection**

Sea Fury VZ345 was used as a pilot training aircraft for a short time; it is seen here over The Needles on 17th April 1985. Crown Copyright / A&AEE Boscombe Down

After the long investigation into the cause of LF363's accident, the RAF then began what was to be an even longer quest to obtain Treasury approval for funds to repair the aircraft and return it to flying condition. By this time, the Service was in the midst of the Government's 'Options for Change' and 'Front Line First' defence initiatives, and despite the RAF's determination to see LF363 back in the air it was necessary for some hard decisions to be taken to raise the funds needed for the Hurricane. The outcome was the most reluctant decision to offer one of the BBMF's Spitfires for sale on the open market, and the choice fell on Mk.XIX PS853, which was duly offered for sale at an auction by Sotheby's on 26th November 1994, where it was knocked down for the sum of £410,000. The sale subsequently fell through, and post-auction negotiations brought about the purchase of PS853 to a then un-named individual. The deal was finally announced on 13th February 1995. The aircraft was flown from Coningsby to its new home four days later and was allotted from the RAF on sale to Euan English, a much respected pilot and operator of historic aircraft, on 21st February. Two days later, PS853 was registered to Euan as G-MXIX. Tragically, Euan did not enjoy ownership of the Spitfire for long, when he was killed while flying his Harvard IIA G-TEAC on 4th March. The civilian future for PS853 is as yet undetermined.

Beyond 1995

During 1995 the nation commemorated the 50th anniversary of the ending of the Second World War, and an essential part of that activity was the participation of the BBMF. Despite the uncertainty caused by the accident to the Hurricane and the sale of PS853, the staff of the Flight were determined to ensure that the display tasking was met in full, so that the nation was able to see the RAF's living memorial to those thousands of aircrew it lost during that now distant conflict. The BBMF and its aircraft are as much the nation's as the RAF's; indeed, they belong to everyone because they are part of our heritage. More so than at any other time, during 1995 and beyond the motto of the Battle of Britain Memorial Flight will be on the lips of everyone who sees its historic aircraft grace the sky – Lest We Forget.

The sad remains of LF363 at Wittering on 11th September 1991; its pilot had a lucky escape. Ken Ellis collection

At the time of its intended sale in November 1995, PS853 carried the markings of 16 Squadron with which it operated in Germany in the years immediately after the war. MAP

MAINTAINING THE MEMORIAL

'It has been suggested, and not altogether in jest, that we should still have a Hurricane and Spitfire flying at the 50th anniversary of the Battle of Britain.'
HQ Strike Command Engineering Review, February 1971.

During every display season, the aircraft of the BBMF appear at countless air shows and other events throughout the country and overseas too. It is remarkable that, all these years after they were built, aircraft which saw active service during the Second World War should still be airworthy and able to appear in public to the delight of so many generations of people.

This achievement is made all the more remarkable when one considers that aircraft such as the Hurricane, the Spitfire and the Lancaster were built in the knowledge that their life expectancy in battle was likely to be very short. Indeed, a large number of aircraft were lost within their first few combat operations, especially during the Battle of Britain itself. As a result, little attention was paid to corrosion protection during assembly, nor were some of the most long-lived materials used in the design. More fundamental from an airworthiness perspective, the concept of structural fatigue was not understood and no fatigue testing was carried out to establish a safe life for the airframes.

With the raised expectations and increasingly litigious nature of modern society, the RAF has had to shoulder the burden of responsibility for maintaining the airworthiness of all its aircraft, including those of the BBMF which are treated little differently from the Flight's Tornado bedfellows at Coningsby. The Flight therefore has a small but vital cadre of 18 permanent staff, led by a Warrant Officer, to tend the aircraft. Whilst there is always a waiting list of volunteers from which to select replacement technicians, it is not always easy to find people with the right skills. For example, the RAF ended its own training in piston engines many years ago, so it has been necessary for a number of BBMF people to attend specially provided courses at CSE Aviation at Oxford Airport, to learn that essential knowledge.

The complexity of the task facing a newly arrived engine technician, for example, is huge, when it is realised that the Flight's aircraft are fitted with some six different variants of the Rolls-Royce Merlin engine alone. Formal on-the-job training is given to everyone, but it might take six or nine months, perhaps even longer, for every new arrival to encounter the full spectrum of tasks in their trade specialisation.

Eventually, each technician must become sufficiently skilled to be able to work with the minimum of direct supervision, which is an important consideration when the aircraft have to be supported away from home. To ease this assimilation task, the majority of the Flight's maintenance schedules have been rewritten into the modern format, as used on the Tornado, so that at least the layout of the maintenance documentation is familiar to the new arrivals.

To ensure that the aircraft are in the peak of condition for the display season, and that they will need little scheduled maintenance during the busy summer months, all of the Flight's aircraft undergo substantial work during the winter. Again, the maintenance philosophy applied to the BBMF fleet owes much to that applied to the front line aircraft, especially in terminology, although the restrictions placed on the number of hours flown each year results in a much shorter flying period between servicings than that allowed for the modern aircraft. The servicing with the smallest content is called a Primary servicing, which is carried out after 30 hours flying, or every four months, whichever comes sooner. During the winter the fighters undergo a Primary 'Star' servicing, which looks much more deeply at the aircraft than the Primary. Every second winter the fighters are given a Minor servicing, which is deeper still, before they go away for a Major servicing every sixth year.

The seemingly smooth nature of the scheduled servicing programme was born out of bitter experience, having evolved from the old wartime requirements that were followed until the early 1960s. By the time the Flight began to attain more formal recognition at Coltishall in the late 1960s, the servicing schedules had been changed from the old flying hour basis to one based on the annual display season. For example, the old minor servicing scheduled to be carried out every 100 hours was reprogrammed to be done yearly, whilst the major was planned to be carried out every four years. Further bitter experience followed a protracted Major servicing carried out on Spitfire Mk.VB AB910 at Coltishall between November 1969 and December 1971, which brought the realisation that it was not feasible to expect the meagre manpower of the Flight to carry out major servicings as well as the routine day-to-day maintenance activities. Although the servicing carried out on AB910 was extremely

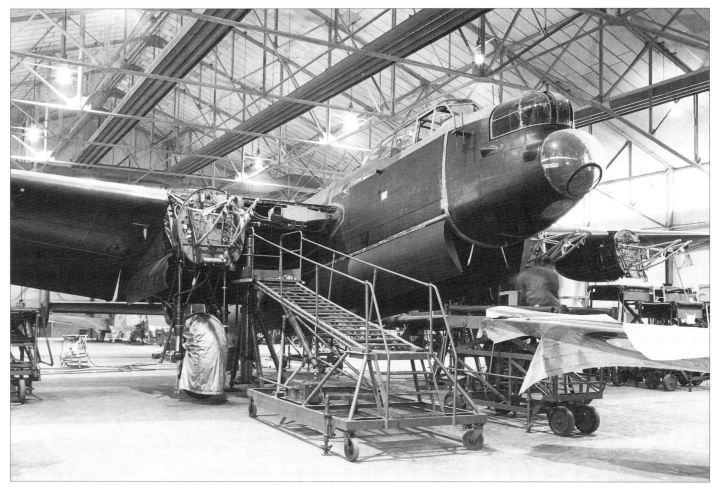

comprehensive, and the aircraft returned fully serviceable at the end of its air test, the conditions under which it was carried out were far from ideal. With only seven servicing personnel on the Flight at the time, it was found impossible to maintain any servicing continuity on the aircraft because tradesmen were regularly interrupted to deal with defects on the flying aircraft which had to be rectified immediately to meet display commitments.

With this experience in mind, in November 1970 the Ministry of Defence agreed to a Hurricane major servicing being carried out in Maintenance Command. This decision was taken because of the availability of specialists to repair the wooden rear fuselage structure, the availability of specialist machine tools and fabrication facilities, and the ability to give continuity of personnel on the task, which was estimated to be in the order of 1,500 to 2,000 man-hours. As a result of the success of this task, Maintenance Command, later RAF Support Command, was tasked to carry out all of the Flight's major servicings. Thereafter, majors were all carried out at 5 Maintenance Unit (MU), Kemble, Gloucestershire, but when that unit's RAF task was run down at the end of 1983, another way had to be found to carry out the work.

A further trial was carried out on the Hurricanes over the winter of 1983-84 whereby

Opposite page: **PA474 nears the end of its winter servicing at Coningsby in February 1983.** Paddy Porter collection

The BBMF's groundcrew at Coltishall on 15th December, 1966. Then six in number, and seen here with their engineer officer, the Flight now fields 18 technicians. Author's collection

PZ865 outside the Flight's hangar for engine runs in August 1976. Paddy Porter collection

the work was once again carried out by the Flight's personnel at Coningsby, but again the additional work could not be finished in the available time by the small complement of permanent manpower. The extent of the additional work required was considerable, with a major on the fighters by this time consuming an average of some 2,500 man-hours, whilst a major on the Lancaster was likely to require some 7,500 man-hours.

It was therefore decided to put the work out to civilian contract, and one of the first such contracts was the major servicing of the Lancaster by West Country Air Services at Exeter Airport, Devon, over the winter of 1987-88. Subsequently, several organisations have carried out winter overhauls on the BBMF aircraft, including the College of Aeronautics at Cranfield, Bedfordshire, Lovaux at Bournemouth Airport, Dorset, and Rolls-Royce at Filton, Avon.

In recent years the RAF's own Maintenance Group at St Athan, South Glamorgan, has been operating on a commercial basis, and it too has tendered for and won overhaul work from the BBMF in direct competition with industry. For example, the Lancaster underwent major servicing at St Athan over the winter 1993-94, whilst P7350 was also serviced at St Athan over the winter 1994-95. The major servicing carried out on the Lancaster at St Athan extended over a period of almost six months and occupied a team of some 20 men drawn from all areas of St Athan's vast organisation.

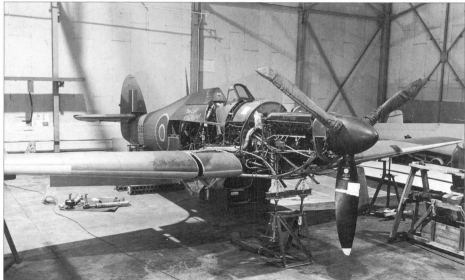

AB910 seen in the midst of its winter servicing at Coningsby in January 1983.

With its undercarriage legs removed for servicing, PZ865 during winter servicing in January 1983. Both Paddy Porter collection

On arrival at St Athan in October 1993, PA474 had flown some 3,850 hours and the purpose of the major servicing was to provide it with a thorough inspection and restoration of its structure and equipment. This involved considerable dismantling, including the removal of all of the engines, fuel tanks, turrets and much of the internal equipment. One particularly large task carried out at St Athan was the total rewiring of the aircraft to modern standards of safety using modern materials, which should result in better safety and greater reliability, with future repairs being carried out much more cheaply.

Throughout the major, the staff at St Athan worked very closely with British Aerospace (BAe), which retains responsibility as the Design Authority for the Lancaster. BAe has a huge library of drawings for the aircraft, although as part of the rewire, St Athan produced a full set of computerised electrical installation drawings for it. Such application of modern maintenance standards and techniques to the historic aircraft of the BBMF can only augur well for their continued ability to remain airworthy. Indeed, at the time of writing, St Athan was preparing an aggressive bid to meet the tender for the forthcoming spar replacement task on PA474.

Having noted the forthcoming need to replace part of the rear spar on the Lancaster, it must be remembered that the BBMF's aircraft are regarded as the fleet leaders in terms of flying hours, and all are maintained on-condition without any finite life applied to the airframes. As a result, every aircraft is inspected very carefully, with everyone looking for structural and other faults before they become a hazard to airworthiness. Not only do the airframes need caring for, but so do the many individual components to be found in the aircraft systems. To enable it to tackle many of these jobs also, the BBMF has installed a hydraulic test bay to test all hydraulic components, whilst propellers and engine parts are serviced and tested in-house before fitting to the aircraft. Further support, especially for electrical components, is provided from the Engineering and Supply Wing at Coningsby.

Spare Part Availability

Perhaps one of the most difficult problems to face the Flight's engineers is the dwindling supply of spare parts, which become ever harder to find as time passes and as more Spitfires especially are made airworthy in civilian hands. Whilst it is quite easy to obtain newly-made airframe parts, these are seldom if ever needed by the BBMF. Usually it is a component that will cause problems, as has been the case in the past with a number of key items. A typical problem to exercise the mind of the engineers in 1970 was the availability of exhaust stubs for the Hurricane LF363, which at the time was fitted with a Merlin Mk.502 which had originated in an Avro York transport. Only one type of stub would clear the engine cowling, but these were only available for the right hand side of the engine. To overcome the problem, a set of right hand stubs were cut down, inverted and rewelded to fit on the left hand side of the engine. However, this improvisation resulted in the left hand stubs pointing upwards, which made things very noisy for the pilot, and there was some risk of ingestion of exhaust fumes into the cockpit.

At times such improvisation by the engineers was often the only way to keep the aircraft flying, and for a period in the early 1970s LF363 was seen sporting a very non-standard four-bladed propeller whilst its own three-blader was overhauled. It is a tribute to the BBMF's organisation and to the support it receives from throughout the RAF and industry that such extremes of improvisation have not been necessary of late. Fortunately, the BBMF has enjoyed considerable support from the aerospace industry, especially from companies such as Rolls-Royce, Dowty-Rotol and British Aerospace. Many of the original manufacturers of equipment for the aircraft have often come to the aid of the Flight, with companies such as Dunlop fashioning replacement rubber bags for use in the pneumatic brake units. Dunlop also produced a special batch of tyres for the smaller Spitfires, whilst in the early 1970s the Mk.XIXs were flying with HS Buccaneer nosewheel tyres fitted to their mainwheels.

Frequently a number of components have to be manufactured, and during the protracted major servicing on AB910, St Athan manufactured a set of replacement wing attachment bolts whilst the Station Workshops at Coltishall, Norfolk, also carried out a great deal of work, including the manufacture of new undercarriage pivot bushes. Additionally, the Flight was given authority to rob parts from the many Spitfires that were then to be found as gate guardians throughout the country.

Following the decision to conduct the BBMF's major servicings within Maintenance Command, later RAF Support Command, 5 MU at Kemble was chosen as the location for much of the work.
Paddy Porter collection

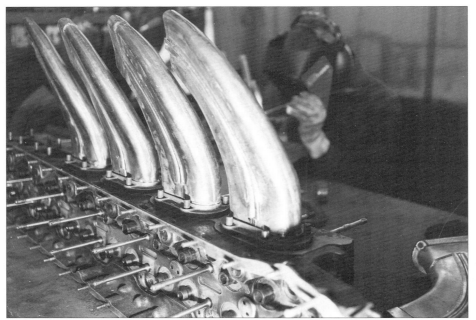

On the operational front, wear and tear on the aircraft was reduced by the flying limitations placed on them, which included no inverted flight, no instrument flying, a minimum runway length of 1,000 yards with operations from grass runways prohibited, no night flying and a maximum crosswind limit of ten knots.

Safe yet Historic

Authenticity is a key feature of the engineering support philosophy for the aircraft, especially as far as the internal equipment is concerned. Indeed, the Flight will go to great effort to obtain old but original equipment to properly equip the aircraft. However, where safety or reliability is concerned, then more modern materials or techniques are accepted. For example, the electrical systems of all the aircraft have now been modified to 24 volt standard because of the increasing difficulty of finding components rated at 12 volts. This change has also eased the ground support problems, because most modern military aircraft incorporate a 24-28 volt electrical system, and the BBMF can find suitable ground power trolleys at most airfields.

Finding some of the original materials for use in repairs is an on-going problem, and modern alternatives often have to be found. In these cases, the modern equivalents invariable have a higher specification than the original, and care must be exercised to ensure the compatibility of old and new. Other key areas where modern equipment has taken over from the original includes the radios and electrical wiring and the air-

Although officially known as a Major servicing, whilst at Cranfield during the winter of 1986/87, LF363 underwent something closer to a complete rebuild. Cranfield University

Detail repair and manufacture is one of St Athan's strengths, as illustrated by this work in progress on Merlin engine exhaust stubs. Author's collection

craft are now fitted with accelerometers to measure the 'g' loads in flight. Perhaps the most outward sign of modern materials is the use of gloss polyurethane paint; although not authentic, it does provide superior corrosion protection and is easier to keep clean.

Griffon Engine Replacement

Authenticity proved impossible to maintain when the Griffon Mk.66 engines in the Mk.XIX Spitfires began to run out of life. The problem was foreseen long before it became critical, and it was decided to adapt the Griffon Mk.58 from Avro Shackletons for use in the Spitfire. Whilst nominally the same engine, there were many problems to be overcome before the re-engining programme could go ahead, and to help the design part of the project Spitfire F.21 LA255 displayed by 1 Squadron at Wittering, near Stamford, was delivered to Coltishall on 25th September 1974, to help with a trial installation. With the assistance of the Central Servicing Development Establishment (CSDE), it was concluded that it was not possible to fit the Griffon Mk.58 into the Spitfire airframe because the supercharger casing fouled the engine bearers.

However, in 1977 the BBMF and the CSDE looked at the problem again, on the assumption that the fouling problem could be overcome by machining of the supercharger casing. Further investigation was carried out by the engineering staff of the Flight, by Coningsby's Aircraft Engineering Squadron and by the CSDE using Spitfire Mk.XIX PS915, which was delivered to Coningsby from display duties at Brawdy, Dyfed, on 7th October 1977. This later work confirmed that by machining the volute casing of the supercharger, and removing the rear slinging point castings from the rocker covers, fouling of the engine bearers would be overcome and Rolls-Royce at East Kilbride in Scotland undertook to evaluate the modified engine and redesign the reduction gear to provide a single propeller output shaft.

Improvisation was often required in the Flight's earlier days, with LF363 sporting a four-bladed propeller at Mildenhall on 22nd May 1971. Author

The ubiquitous 'trolley acc' provides ground electrical power for engine starting with the fleet now fully converted to 24-volt electrical systems. Paddy Porter collection

On the assumption that the design work by Rolls-Royce would clear the proposed modifications to the engine, the trials work at Coningsby went on to look at the many other areas of the engine installation that would have to be modified to complete the installation. This work included modifications to the throttle control linkage, replacement of hoses and pipelines in the fuel, oil and coolant systems, and various other changes to the ignition system, starter system, exhaust stubs, the engine air intake and cowlings and the cockpit instrumentation. Much of the work was relatively minor in nature and within the capability of the BBMF's own resources or those of the station, although some elements of the work had to be carried out at St Athan. With its trial installation work complete, PS915 was moved to the Sergeants' Mess at Coningsby on 15th September 1978, where it was displayed for a period of a year or so before being returned to Brawdy on 25th March 1980.

Having proved that the project was viable, work began to install the first Griffon Mk.58 into the BBMF's Mk.XIX PS853, which was found to have engine problems during its major servicing at Kemble in 1981. The aircraft was returned to Coningsby by road on 19th September whereupon there began an extensive programme of work to modify the engine compartment to accept the new engine. However, such was the complexity of the work and the availability of personnel that it was to be almost a decade later before PS853 would next fly, which it did on 20th July 1989, fitted with its new engine.

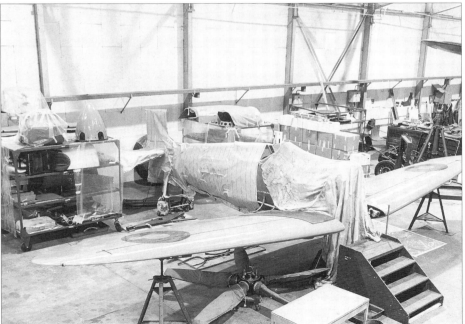

As part of the Griffon re-engining scheme, PS915 left its Brawdy display duties to act as the trial installation airframe.
C F E Smedley

PS853 'hibernates' during the long wait for the development of its new engine installation. Paddy Porter collection

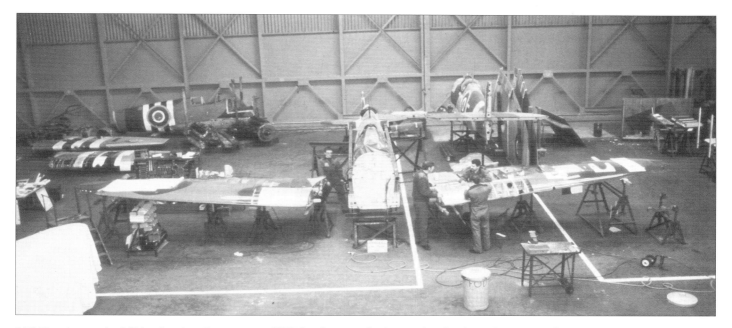

AB910 under repair at Abingdon, together with donor airframes MK732 (left) and BL614 (right). Author's collection

Maintenance Assistance

The BBMF takes its airworthiness responsibilities very seriously indeed, and is able to call on the resources of organisations from both within and outside the RAF for help and advice. Foremost of the external agencies the Flight deals with are British Aerospace and Rolls Royce, who in essence were the manufacturers of the aircraft and their engines. From within the service, one of the key agencies is the CSDE, until early 1995 located at Swanton Morley, Norfolk, and now moved principally to Wyton, Cambridgeshire, to form part of the Logistics Support Services organisation. By far the most regularly used element of the CSDE is the Non-Destructive Testing Squadron, now located at St Athan, which has been called in on many occasions to carry out X-ray or other structural inspection work.

CSDE has been at the heart of maintaining the structural integrity of the aircraft, which is the key to their continued ability to fly, and structural surveys have long been a feature of the maintenance programme for all of the Flight's aircraft. The aim of the structural surveys, which were first carried out by the CSDE at Kemble whilst the aircraft were stripped down for major servicing, was to assess the condition of the structure in areas not normally accessible for structural examination during scheduled servicing.

Special techniques such as x-ray testing and visual inspection using endoprobes were used to gain a comprehensive assessment of the condition of each aircraft, knowledge which was used to plan the forthcoming five-year maintenance programme. Generally, the aircraft were found to be in good condition, although a number of husbandry measures were recommended to ensure their continued safe operation.

Lancaster Structural Repairs

It is the Lancaster's structure that has probably suffered the most, the aircraft perhaps having spent a lot of its life parked out in the open in various parts of the world. For example, over the winter of 1970-71, a structural survey found PA474 in surprisingly good condition, but the electrical wiring was found to be very poor and much of it needed renewal.

However, during the Lancaster's winter servicing in 1977-78, corrosion was found in the rivets of the engine nacelles, the flaps and the underside of the wings where they were affected by exhaust gases from the engines. This work was carried out at Coningsby by personnel on detachment from Abingdon, Oxfordshire, in a long programme which kept the Lancaster on the ground for more than a year. Further repairs to bolt holes in the main spar and corrosion in the mainplanes were carried out at Abingdon between November 1980 and April 1981.

Now 50 years old, maintaining the structural integrity of the Lancaster requires a constant programme of inspection and repair. Here a tailplane receives attention to rivets and corrosion. C F E Smedley

After its accident at Coltishall in November 1972, the starboard wing from AB910 was sent to Bicester for repair by 71 MU. Neville Franklin collection

Another structural survey was carried out on the Lancaster during the following winter, from which a progressive programme of husbandry was developed. One benefit to flow from the continued structural integrity programme on the aircraft has been the extension of the major servicing from a four-year to a six-year cycle, which has resulted in considerable savings in support costs with no reduction in airworthiness standards.

Whilst most of the major improvements in the modification standard of the BBMF's aircraft are made when the aircraft are away from Coningsby, many quite large modifications are still embodied during the minor servicings which are carried out by the Flight's own personnel. Over the winter of 1989-90, for example, Spitfire Mk.VB AB910 was totally rewired and its electrical system was upgraded to 24 volt capacity, whilst Hurricane LF363 had long range fuel tanks installed to bring its fuel capacity up to that of PZ865.

Repairs After Accidents

Ensuring the continued structural integrity of such historical aircraft is clearly a headache for the engineers, but coping with the effects of an accident can bring many extra problems. The Flight's aircraft have suffered a number of minor bumps and bruises, often caused by undercarriage or engine problems. Unfortunately, there have also been a small number of more serious accidents.

One of the earliest and best publicised accidents to afflict the Flight was the engine failure which befell Spitfire Mk.XVI SL574 over Bromley, Kent, on 20th September 1959, whilst being flown in the annual Battle of Britain flypast over London. More recently, engine problems on take-off saw Spitfire Mk.IIA P7350 overshoot the end of the runway at Chivenor, Devon, on 29th July 1992, and tip onto its nose, again without injury to the pilot and only minor damage to the aircraft.

A number of other minor accidents have occurred, including an undercarriage failure on AB910 following a ground-loop at Coltishall in October 1972, which resulted in its right-hand wing being sent to 71 MU at Bicester, Oxfordshire, for repair. AB910 suffered another undercarriage failure on landing at Duxford, Cambridgeshire, on 26th June 1976, when a torque link failed and the aircraft tipped up onto its nose and right wingtip. A further undercarriage failure occurred on LF363 at Northolt, Greater London, in September 1976, whilst it was flying with the propeller and spinner from PZ865. Thankfully, the Lancaster has not suffered such an accident record, although strong cross-winds during landing at Mildenhall, Suffolk, in May 1992 did see it make an unplanned excursion onto the grass, necessitating some careful checks of the undercarriage following its safe return to Coningsby. More recently, the Lancaster veered off the runway at Brussels and as a precaution the undercarriage legs were sent to Dowty for checking during the winter servicing 1994-95 to ensure that all was well.

There have, however, been two serious accidents to aircraft of the BBMF which have resulted in extensive repair work being required. The first of these again involved Spitfire Mk.VB AB910, and occurred at Bex in Switzerland on 21st August 1978.

AB910 after its ground-loop at Coltishall in November 1972. Paddy Porter collection

AB910 was extensively damaged and it was taken to 5 MU, Kemble, on 6th September to await a decision on its repair. There was considerable damage to the engine bulkhead and wings and the rear fuselage skin was badly buckled but it was decided to go ahead and repair the aircraft, which was taken to Abingdon for the work to be carried out. During the repair, various components were removed from Spitfire Mk.IX MK732, which was delivered from St Athan to Abingdon during September 1979 to assist as a donor airframe. On 8th January 1980, a second Spitfire, Mk.VB BL614, was also taken to Abingdon to act as a reference item in the final stages of the repair. With the repair completed, AB910 was returned by road to 5 MU for a major servicing, reassembly and painting. It returned to its base at Coningsby on 23rd October 1981.

The most recent, and most serious, accident to involve an aircraft of the Flight was that which occurred to Hurricane LF363 on 11th September 1991. The wreckage was taken to Coningsby, where it languished for some time whilst the RAF found a way to fund the repair that would be acceptable to the Treasury.

With the deepest regret, the only solution open to the RAF was to put Spitfire Mk.XIX PS853 on the market to raise the money required, and tenders were sought from the civilian warbird industry to rebuild LF363. The repair contract was awarded to Historic Flying Ltd, and LF363 was moved to Audley End, Essex, for the work to begin on 6th September 1994. However, the extensive work required was not expected to be completed before the summer of 1996.

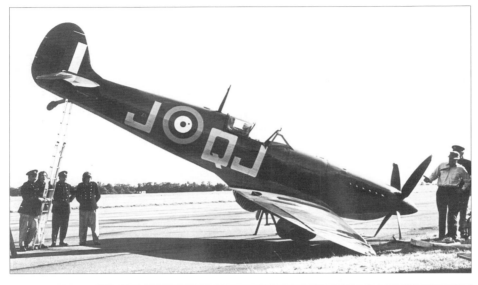

The winter maintenance programme on each aircraft is really an investment for the future, both in the long term integrity of the aircraft, but also in their reliability for the forthcoming display season. The pressure to have every aircraft available every weekend is considerable, especially in the case of the Lancaster, Hurricane and Dakota, where the BBMF has only one of each type, although with the Spitfires there is a little more flexibility.

There are also busy times of the year, for example the annual Battle of Britain weekend, or the D-Day and Arnhem commemorations during 1994, when a special effort is made to ensure that every commitment is met.

That few display tasks are lost because of unserviceability underlines the effort made by the Flight's incredibly small workforce to ensure that the public is not disappointed. It is also clear that the tender loving care devoted to these historic aircraft will see them remain airworthy for many years to come.

Opposite page:

Failure of the starboard undercarriage pintle on landing at Duxford in June 1976 caused this second accident to AB910.

The Hurricanes have not been free from incident, as illustrated by LF363's undercarriage failure at Northolt in September 1976.
Both Paddy Porter collection

Some three years after the crash at Wittering, LF363 awaits the healing treatment at Historic Flying Ltd's Audley End hangar.
Steve Hague via Ken Ellis

A tense moment at the end of the winter servicing comes when the engines are started again for the first time. Here PA474 is the centre of attention as it is reawakened on 20th April 1979 after a quadruple engine change and major structural repairs which saw it grounded throughout 1978. C F E Smedley

DISPLAY DUTY

It is no exaggeration to say that the BBMF is in itself a memorial, a living memorial which translates into a tangible form the respects of a grateful nation for that small band of pilots which fought so valiantly during the Battle of Britain, just as the Lancaster does for those thousands of bomber crews who lost their lives during the bombing campaign of the Second World War. The BBMF maintains its aircraft in flying condition as a tribute to those who gave their lives in them but, more importantly, the BBMF can also present those aircraft in their natural environment for the greater enjoyment of the general public. As a result, every year there are many hundreds of applications for the BBMF to display, at events ranging from the largest air shows to bomber squadron reunions and village fetes.

Unfortunately, with the ever-pressing constraint on resources, it is just not possible for the Flight to meet every request, and to sort order out of what might otherwise become chaos, a Participation Committee sits in the Ministry of Defence in London before the end of each year to consider all the bids and to decide the allocation of the principal display teams, such as the BBMF and the Red Arrows, for the following year.

The allocation is made in full consultation with the Flight, with the aim that as many displays as possible will be carried out within the available flying time on the aircraft, although pilot training has a high priority within the permitted hours. By Christmas, therefore, the broad framework of the following year's display programme has been worked out and in the new year the detailed planning can begin.

Typically, the display season will begin in April and end after the RAF's principal Battle of Britain displays in September, by which

Above: **Making its distinctive curved approach, LF363 comes in to land in the days before 'bone-domes' became essential wear for pilots.** Robert Rudhall

Opposite page left: **PA474, flanked by AB910 and LF363, overflying Waddington on 5th March 1968 during rehearsals for the ceremonies to mark the formation of Strike Command. This was one of the first occasions when Waddington's Lancaster and the aircraft of the Battle of Britain Flight at Coltishall were teamed for a display.** Rolls-Royce via Neville Franklin

time the Flight will have performed some 400 individual displays at almost 300 venues. The achievement of the BBMF is quite remarkable when compared with the scale of the Red Arrows, which have a similar number of aircraft but carry out only half the number of displays.

The Display Year
Planning the yearly programme is further eased because many of the major events are of long standing, such as the Air Fete at Mildenhall which has been held over the bank holiday at the end of May for many years now, and the venue is therefore well known to the pilots. That said, every detail is double-checked to ensure that nothing has changed, especially that no new masts or

other obstructions have been built, or that there has been no change to adjacent sensitive areas, such as schools, hospitals and stables. Where the display venue is new, more preparation is required, especially if it is at an off-airfield site. In these cases it is quite likely that the route will be flown in advance of the display date using the DHC Chipmunk to ensure that on the day itself the display aircraft approach from the right direction for maximum effect. During 1994, much thought was given to the drop of poppy petals to be made by PA474 at the D-Day commemoration, such that drop trials were carried out over the Wainfleet bombing range to perfect the technique; once again, the Chipmunk was used to preview the route before the Lancaster was flown.

Several types of display go to make up the BBMF's varied programme, ranging from what might be termed the mandatory appearances at the RAF's own Battle of Britain air shows, although now few in number, plus displays at significant events of national importance. During 1994 the latter task included the D-Day and Arnhem commemorations, whilst in 1995 the Flight was fully committed to the many events held to commemorate VE Day. Each year seems to see more and more air shows throughout the United Kingdom, and the Participation Committee will attach high priority to the Flight's attendance at such significant locations as Mildenhall, the Biggin Hill Air Fair and the International Air Tattoo at Fairford where large crowds are expected.

Thereafter, it becomes largely a matter of judgement – should a minor event coincide with one of the major shows, the Flight might have the opportunity to carry out an additional display or perhaps just a flypast on the way to or from the main event. Following detailed scrutiny of the bids for each weekend, it might be possible for the flight to attend three major displays, with the opportunity of also putting in an appearance with one or more aircraft at up to five suitably located minor events.

The number of displays attended by the BBMF has grown considerably from the lean years of the 1960s until in 1994 displays were planned at 294 venues, of which 254 were flown as planned, the others being lost largely due to weather restrictions. At the time of writing the BBMF's 1995 flying programme comprised over 300 display venues. Much of the planned increase was the result of the VE Day commemoration events, although the Lancaster was expected to visit the Netherlands to mark the 50th anniversary of Operation MANNA, the dropping of relief supplies to the Dutch people in early 1945. Because of the imminent need to respar the Lancaster, the BBMF was hoping to fly off the aircraft's remaining hours to ensure that the public gained the maximum benefit from its available life.

Whilst the aims and intentions of the BBMF are clear, there are many factors which often impose constraints on what can be achieved despite the most meticulous planning. Perhaps the greatest variable is the weather, because a cloud base of 1,500 ft and a visibility of not less than 5 km is required to allow a display to go ahead. The wind can impose further restrictions, depending on where the aircraft will be taking off or landing. Crosswinds are the concern, with a 15 kt limit imposed for take-off and a 10 kt limit for landing, although given a wind on the nose during take-off and landing, operations are permitted up to wind speeds of 25 kt. Rain is something else, which must be avoided if at all possible because of the damage that can be caused by erosion, especially to the leading edges of the propeller blades. The sound basis for prudent weather limitations was clearly illustrated in May 1992 when the Lancaster departed from the runway at Mildenhall in a gusting wind, fortunately without damage.

Training

Attaining and maintaining the competency of the pilots is a key feature of the BBMF's *modus operandi* and before the start of the season every pilot must work-up on his allocated aircraft, although the Chipmunk is available throughout the year for them to keep in 'taildragging' practice. The currency requirement for the pilots is to fly five hours 'taildragger' per month, and the Chipmunk has an allowance of 180 hours per year for this. New pilots joining the Flight first fly 25 hours in the Chipmunk before going to Boscombe Down, Wiltshire, for two sorties in the North American Harvard. After that they solo on the Hurricane which they must fly for a minimum of 15 hours before graduating to the Merlin-engined Spitfires. Once on the 'baby' Spitfires, a new pilot must fly another 15 hours before moving up to the Griffon-powered Mk.XIXs, which usually occurs in the second year.

A further constraint on the new pilot is that he would not be allowed to participate in the synchronised manoeuvres until about mid-way through the first season, subject to the approval of the Flight's training officer, who controls all pilot conversion and continuation training.

Training for the Lancaster pilots is provided throughout the year by the Dakota, which does give good experience in flying a large 'taildragger' although it is much easier to handle than the Lancaster. However, there is no substitute for flying the real thing, and the Lancaster is allowed ten hours per year for training. Once competent in the aircraft, each pilot must have his display routine cleared for public exhibition, first by the Station Commander and then by the Air Officer Commanding 11 Group, under whose command the BBMF operates.

Display Routine

Detailed planning for a specific airshow will begin several weeks in advance, as it may take some time to work out the myriad of arrangements needed to support the aircraft and the personnel. Generally, when it is necessary to land at a venue, the Flight aims to deploy on a Friday afternoon, which gives the Saturday morning for a second chance if there have been problems with the weather or serviceability. When the aircraft land for a night stop, it is a condition placed on the show organisers that hangarage be provided for the Spitfires or the Hurricane – the Lancaster and Dakota stay in the open – and groundcrew to support the event travel either in the Lancaster or the Dakota. Prior to the arrival of the Dakota, the Devon was used in this support role, which provided greater flexibility than having to rely totally on the ever-helpful SAL Jetstreams from Finningley.

The BBMF overflies to mark the annual ceremony where RAF Coningsby exercises its Freedom of the Borough of Boston.
Paddy Porter collection

The transit flight from Coningsby to the display venue brings problems of its own, particularly as the aircraft are almost totally devoid of the array of modern navigation equipment always found in current jet fighters. Navigation is performed by map reading and timing, although more modern avionics equipment is now being fitted to the aircraft to improve their safe operation. Typical of the new equipment starting to appear in the aircraft are transponders, which give ground radar control centres a precise readout of aircraft height, and V/UHF radios, which allow the pilots to communicate with both civil and military establishments.

The BBMF prefers to transit direct to the venue, to reduce non-productive flying time, rather than be diverted around controlled airspace. Air traffic control centres, both civil and military, do everything that they can to clear a route for the usual formation of Lancaster, Hurricane and Spitfire. However, one of the pilots did wryly remark that the Chipmunk did not seem to get quite the same standard of service!

Transit flights are conducted under visual flight rules, generally at a height of between 2,000 and 3,000 ft. As might be expected, the Dakota has sufficient instruments for flight in the civil airways. Interestingly, the Devon is preferred as the escort aircraft because it can motor along at 175 knots, a comfortable speed for the fighters, whilst the Dakota rumbles along a little too slowly.

Once at the venue, a seemingly endless series of briefings begins to ensure that the public are treated to a safe but interesting display. Given the strict controls placed on airshows by the Civil Aviation Authority (CAA), the briefings usually start with one for all of the participating pilots conducted by the show organiser.

Such briefing sessions will include details of procedures specific to the show, weather conditions, changes to timings or running order and emergency procedures. That completed, the BBMF pilots then hold their own private briefing, especially important where formation and synchronised manoeuvres are to be carried out. In this briefing, the weather and other details are reiterated, and then the sequence to be flown that day is briefed. Particular emphasis is placed on engine start, taxi and take-off instructions which might be critical on a hot day if overheating of the big water-cooled piston engines is to be avoided. The display sequence would then be briefed, together with join-up and departure details. In the event that a second display or flypast was to be carried out on the way back to Coningsby, that would be briefed also. Whilst the aircrew carry out the essential flight planning and briefing, the groundcrew would make the aircraft ready for flight, ensuring that the necessary fuel and oil were aboard.

Once airborne and happy with the serviceability of the aircraft, the BBMF formation normally holds until the allotted display

Hurricane PZ865 rests in the shadow of the Lancaster before taking part in the flying display at Wyton on 16th July 1973.
Paddy Porter collection

time. Generally, if the Flight is displaying its three principal types, the routine will last for some 12 to 15 minutes, with each aircraft allocated up to five minutes. In some cases, the fighters will not display individually, but as a synchronised pair. Recently there has been a tendency towards less three-ship displays with the Spitfires taking on a greater share of the work.

In addition to the routine, the pilots must observe strict performance limitations imposed on the aircraft. Under normal operations, the fighters are permitted to apply up to three 'g', with a never-exceed limit of four 'g'. The Lancaster, on the other hand, is limited to 1.8 'g'; and is fitted with a fatigue meter which faithfully records every application of stress on the airframe for future analysis. Similarly, airspeeds are strictly limited; 275 kts maximum, with engine boost restricted to +6 for Merlins, +7 for Griffons. These limitations are not the constraint that they might at first appear, although they do prevent a fully developed vertical display of loops and vertical rolls, and they fit neatly with the cloudbase requirement of 1,500 ft which will usually permit a display by the Flight, even on a poor summer's day.

A typical display routine for the BBMF formation would include an arrival from the holding point followed by a 'petal break' in which the Lancaster's fighter escorts would break away to commence the synchronised display of wing-overs and rolls.

Whilst the Lancaster is regularly photographed against a backdrop of Lincoln Cathedral, care is always needed to ensure that the flight is carried out safely.
Paddy Porter collection

Meanwhile, the Lancaster would hold at crowd rear during the fighter display before itself running in for a 360° turn during which the bomb-bay is opened and closed. There then follows a clean turn and a cloverleaf before it begins an approach with the undercarriage and flaps lowered.

Then, with all four Merlins roaring at high power, the Lancaster overshoots from the dummy approach prior to being rejoined by the fighters for a final departure flypast. Where just one aircraft was being displayed, the routine would take some five minutes.

A new item in the Lancaster's repertoire was the 'Poppy Drop', seen for the first time during June 1994, when PA474 dropped a huge cloud of poppy petals over the D-Day commemoration events. In keeping with the high standards of the Flight, the task was first rehearsed over the Wainfleet air weapons range and further poppy drops were expected to be carried out as part of the VE Day schedule.

The founding principle for all of the BBMF's displays is safety, both for the spectators, the aircrew and the historic aircraft. In addition to complying with the RAF's own stringent limitations on the aircraft and their operation, the BBMF pilots also have to comply with CAA requirements if displaying at a civilian location, the aircrew being mindful of the problems which could be caused for show organisers as well as themselves if the rules are broken. The variability of the wind probably causes the most problems during a display, and could result in an infringement of the regulations if the pilot were to allow the aircraft to be blown off track. Keeping to the precise timing is another key concern of the pilots, especially from the safety perspective but also as a matter of professional pride.

The end result of all the preparation, both on the ground and in the air, is a display that is well thought out and demonstrates the highlights of each aircraft in a safe and well-controlled manner. Whenever and wherever the aircraft of the BBMF appear, the spectators stop and look skyward to absorb the sight and the sound of just a small part of the nation's heritage.

P7350 and AB910 bask in the summer sunshine awaiting their turn to display at Coningsby's own air day on 14th June 1986. Author

A new arrival on the BBMF, support Dakota ZA947 was quickly pressed into use as a display item in its own right. Author

PA474 overflies the Derwent Dam as part of a 617 Squadron reunion function.
Paddy Porter collection

Opposite page: **Sporting a four-bladed propeller, PZ865 is seen over the beach near Cromer during 1973. Holiday resorts are regular display venues for the BBMF.**
Paddy Porter collection

PICTORIAL
TRIBUTE

**On 14th September 1962, 111 Squadron at Wattisham celebrated
five generations of fighters with this mixed formation of aircraft
carrying various adaptions of the squadron's black and yellow
markings. From left to right: Hurricane Mk.IIC LF363, Spitfire Mk.XIX
PM631, Meteor F.8 WL181, Hunter F.6 XJ715, Lightning F.1A XM190.**
Robert Rudhall collection

**The BBMF airborne from Coltishall on 5th August 1964 in company
with Lightning F.1As of 56 Squadron and 226 Operational
Conversion Unit.** Peter Green collection

Opposite page:
**Airborne from Biggin Hill on 11th October 1957, Flight Lieutenant
R Irish formates his 41 Squadron Hunter F.5 WN983 on PS853 being
flown by Wing Commander P D Thompson.** Bruce Robertson

Opposite page:

TE476 and LF363 share the apron at West Malling with the Javelins of 85 Squadron, 5th August 1959. Neville Franklin collection

PM631 and LF363 turn round at Little Rissington, October 1965. Ray Coulson

For 1990, Spitfire Mk.VB AB910 was wearing the markings of 41 Squadron as used at the time of the Battle of Britain, carrying the badge and inscription of the Guinea Pig Club. Paddy Porter collection

This page:

All of the BBMF's aircraft took part in the film *The Battle of Britain*, during which they carried a variety of markings. Seen here are Hurricane Mk.IIC PZ865 as 'MI-B' and Spitfire Mk.XIX PS853 as 'EI-K'.
Both Robert Rudhall collection

Before joining the BBMF, Spitfire Mk.XIX PS853 served with the Central Fighter Establishment at Binbrook, where it was involved in a series of flight trials with the Lightnings of the Air Fighting Development Squadron and the Javelins of the resident 64 Squadron. Here the departing CO of AFDS makes a flypast at Binbrook in PS853, 'accompanied' by a Lightning F.3 of AFDS, March 1964. Author's collection

LF363 and AB910, for many years the BBMF's principal display mounts.
Neville Franklin

Seen at Wethersfield on 28th May 1960, PZ865 was without its 'Last of the Many!' inscription, and carried its civil registration G-AMAU in small letters on the fuselage side under the tailplane. C F E Smedley

Before being made airworthy for the Battle of Britain film, P7350 spent many years as a static exhibit at Colerne. Author's collection

When operated by the Central Fighter Establishment, first at West Raynham and then at Binbrook, PS853 carried green and brown camouflage colours; it is seen here at Manby in July 1963. Peter Green

Opposite page:

On arrival at Waddington, PA474 was quickly painted in the colours of 44 Squadron and appeared at the station's Battle of Britain 'At Home' day in September 1965. Author's collection

Having been painted in camouflage colours, LF363 is seen here at Farnborough in the early 1960s. Author's collection

Opposite page:

Top left: **The aircraft of the BBMF appeared in a variety of markings during filming of *The Battle of Britain*. Here PZ865 leads G-AWLW, which later went to Canada.**
Author's collection

Top right: **Proudly bearing the Coat of Arms of the City of Lincoln, PA474 basks in the spring sunshine at Coningsby on 5th May 1979.** C F E Smedley

Bottom: **On joining the BBMF, PZ865 was soon painted in the colours of 257(Burma) Squadron, as flown by Squadron Leader R R Stanford Tuck; the aircraft was photographed in these markings at Wattisham on 18th September 1972.** Author

Above: **P7350 positions for the camera near Thurleigh on 11th September 1979.**
C F E Smedley

**LF363 formates with the Lancaster on the
run-in to Coningsby on 18th May 1980.**
C F E Smedley

Opposite page:

**PZ865 overflies the British Aerospace
factory at Weybridge, the former Brooklands
racing circuit, during November 1985 to
mark the 50th anniversary of the type's first
flight.** British Aerospace

AB910 made a second journey to Cranfield for major servicing and is seen here during flight test in April 1991. Cranfield University

A 'party-piece' worked up to thrill the crowds during 1989 was a formation display with P7350 and a Tornado of the resident 229 OCU. Seen overhead Coningsby on 18th July 1989, the Spitfire was being flown by Squadron Leader Paul Day and the Tornado F.3, in 5 Squadron markings, by Wing Commander Rick Peacock-Edwards. Rick Brewell/DPR (RAF)

For several years the BBMF's support workhorse, Devon VP981 has recently been stored and seems destined for future sale.
Author's collection

On arrival at the BBMF, Dakota ZA947 was repainted in wartime camouflage to commemorate the 1944 airborne landings at Arnhem.
Author's collection

Photograph on page 72:

Nine Squadron old and new. Two Tornados of the present 9 Squadron formate on PA474 off the Lincolnshire coast. In addition to the usual array of drop tanks, pods and Sidewinder missiles, the Tornados are armed with ALARM air launched anti-radar missiles.
Rick Brewell/DPR (RAF)

PS915 on an early test flight over the British Aerospace airfield and plant at Samlesbury during January 1987. British Aerospace

All of the aircraft of the BBMF airborne from Coltishall in the early 1970s, before the arrival of the Lancaster. From front to rear: LF363, PZ865, P7350, AB910, PM631 and PS853. Author's collection

PA474 overflies one of the many disused airfields in Lincolnshire soon after the application of the City of Lincoln Coat of Arms. Author's collection

CODES & MARKINGS

The aircraft of the BBMF have carried a variety of different code letters and markings during their display lives. Each different set of codes or markings has a particular significance. Codes are given in order of appearance on the BBMF aircraft.

Hurricane Mk.IIC LF363

On first becoming a display aircraft, LF363 was repainted in an overall silver colour scheme. However, by the time that the Historic Aircraft Flight came into being in 1957 it had acquired a camouflage colour scheme, without any squadron code letters.

LE-D These code letters were used to commemorate the markings of the aircraft flown by Squadron Leader Douglas Bader's Hurricane on 242 (Canadian) Squadron which was based at Coltishall, Norfolk, and Duxford, Cambridgeshire, during the Battle of Britain. The aircraft has carried these code letters in two different styles, firstly in the 'thin' style, which were applied when the aircraft was repainted at Kemble, Gloucestershire, in April 1969 following its appearance in the Battle of Britain film. However, by 1973, the same code letters had been repainted in the 'thick' style.

How it's done. Hurricane LF363 being sprayed up in 85 Squadron codes at Coningsby in January 1983. Paddy Porter collection.

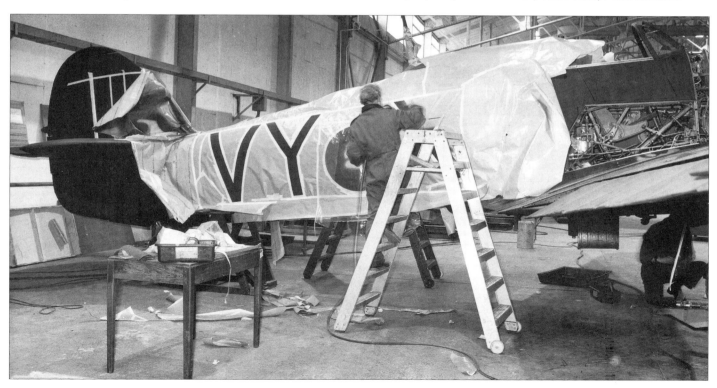

fictitious serial numbers, these included: H3420; H3421; H3422. 'Squadron' code letters worn included: 'MI-A'; 'MI-D'; 'MI-H'; 'KV-C'; 'KV-H'.

Hurricane Mk.IIC PZ865

When built, PZ865 was painted in the standard 1944 camouflage colours. However, when the aircraft was civilianised and registered as G-AMAU, it was painted in the Royal blue and gold colours of HRH The Princess Margaret. Following refurbishment, PZ865 was returned to its original camouflage colour scheme.

'The Last of The Many!' When presented to the BBMF in March 1972, PZ865 carried the standard factory-applied camouflage finish and the inscription 'The Last of the Many!', as was applied to the aircraft on its roll-out at Langley, Buckinghamshire, in 1944. These markings were then reapplied to the aircraft for the 1982 season.

DT-A Some four months after its arrival on the Flight, PZ865 was sent to Kemble on 18th July, 1972, to be repainted in the code letters 'DT-A', to represent the aircraft of 257 (Burma) Squadron as flown by Squadron Leader R R Stanford Tuck from Debden in August and September 1940.

JU-Q The code letters 'JU-Q' were applied to PZ865 during its winter servicing 1977-78 to represent an aircraft of 111 Squadron, the first squadron to operate the Hurricane.

RF-U PZ865 emerged from major servicing with the College of Aeronautics in July 1988 carrying the code letters 'RF-U' of 303 (Polish) Squadron. For the 1989 display season, the aircraft emerged representing the aircraft flown by Sergeant Josef Frantisek, of 303 (Polish) Squadron, the highest scoring fighter pilot of the Battle of Britain period.

GN-F The code letters 'GN-F' represent an aircraft of 249 (Gold Coast) Squadron which operated from Church Fenton Yorkshire, Boscombe Down, Wiltshire, and, by September 1940, from North Weald, Essex. The markings were applied during the major servicing carried out at Kemble during the winter of 1978-79, and were intended to represent the aircraft of Flight Lieutenant E J B Nicolson, who was awarded the Victoria Cross following an action on 16th August, 1940. However, Nicolson's Hurricane, P3576, had been coded 'GN-A'.

VY-X During its winter servicing at Coningsby, Lincolnshire, in January 1983, LF363 was repainted in the black colour scheme and code letters of a Hurricane night fighter of 85 Squadron, which operated from Debden, Essex, during the Battle of Britain. This aircraft was at one time flown by Flight Lieutenant Vashon James Wheeler, who was awarded the Military Cross during the First World War and the Distinguished Flying Cross whilst flying with 85 Squadron during the Second World War. Later he was awarded a Bar to the DFC. Wing Commander V J Wheeler, by then the Commanding Officer of 207 Squadron (Lancasters) based at Spilsby, Lincolnshire, was killed in action during the night of 22nd/23rd March 1944.

NV-L The code letters 'NV-L' represented an aircraft of 79 Squadron during 1940 and were applied to LF363 on completion of its major servicing by the College of Aeronautics at Cranfield, Bedfordshire, in June 1987. No 79 Squadron operated the Hurricane for longer than any other squadron.

GN-A Having earlier wrongly represented the code letters of the aircraft in which Flight Lieutenant E J B Nicolson was awarded the Victoria Cross, for the celebrations to mark the 50th anniversary of the Battle of Britain during 1990, LF363 was repainted in the colours of 249 (Gold Coast) Squadron with the correct code for Nicolson's aircraft, 'GN-A'. The aircraft was wearing these markings when it crashed on 11th September 1991.

US-C It is understood that once LF363 has completed its rebuild at Historic Flying Ltd, Audley End, Essex, in 1996 it will be painted in the markings of 56 Squadron, which is now the reserve squadron number allocated to the Panavia Tornado F.3 conversion unit at Coningsby, which supplies most of the pilots for the BBMF.

Film appearances: During the filming of *The Battle of Britain*, LF363 wore a variety of

J After major servicing by Rolls-Royce at Filton over the winter 1992-93, PZ865 was returned to the BBMF following a complete refabric and repaint in the colours of 261 Squadron (formerly 418 Flight) wearing the individual code letter 'J'. These markings were selected to represent Hurricane I P3731, one of 12 aircraft painted in desert camouflage and flown off HMS *Argus* in Operation HURRY, the relief of Malta, in September 1940. In adopting these markings, the aircraft also represented all those who served with the Middle East Air Force during the Second World War.

Film Appearances: PZ865 carried the spurious markings of P2619 and the code letters 'US-B' of 56 Squadron during its participation in the film *Angels One-Five* in the 1950s. During its participation in the film *The Battle of Britain*, PZ865 wore a variety of serial numbers and code letters, including: H3419; H3421; H3423; H3424, and the codes 'MI-B'; 'MI-C'; 'MI-D'; 'MI-G'; 'KV-A'; 'OK-I'.

Spitfire Mk.IIA P7350

ZH-T The codes 'ZH-T' applied to P7350 represent 266 (Rhodesia) Squadron which operated the aircraft from Wittering during the Battle of Britain, although the code letters 'ZH' were only used by the squadron on Typhoons from March 1942. The markings were applied at 5 MU, Kemble, when the aircraft was serviced and repainted there between 28th April and 12th June 1969, after its participation in the Battle of Britain film. Whilst displayed at Colerne, Wiltshire, before being made airworthy for the film, P7350 first carried just 'ZH' and later 'ZH-T', which is perhaps the source of the confusion in later years.

UO-T Having noted the error in the markings carried by P7350, by 1972 the correct squadron letters 'UO-' had been applied to the aircraft, which retained its correct individual letter T.

'JU-Q', 111 Squadron colours, applied to PZ865 during 1977-78. MAP

With Polish 'chequerboard' on the cowling, PZ865 wore 303 Squadron markings from 1989. MAP

QV-B Following approval of the policy to change the squadron markings depicted by the aircraft of the BBMF, the aircraft was repainted in the markings of 19 Squadron, the first squadron to receive the Spitfire, whilst it underwent major servicing at Kemble over the winter of 1977-78.

SH-D By the time of its return from major servicing at Kemble, which took place between 22nd September 1981 and 26th August 1982, P7350 was repainted into the codes 'SH-D', to represent the aircraft of 64 Squadron. This selection was made at the instigation of the BBMF itself, in recognition of Coningsby being the home of 64 (Reserve) Squadron, which would form from the resident 228 Operational Conversion Unit (OCU) for exercises or in time of war. Many 64(R) Squadron/228 OCU pilots volunteered their time to fly the aircraft of the BBMF during displays.

PZ865 as one of the 'stars' in *Angels One-Five*, 1951. Airspeed Oxford behind. MAP

P7350 in 64 Squadron markings, 1983. MAP

was to carry the codes 'YT-F' in recognition of 65 (East India) Squadron, the reserve squadron number allocated to 229 OCU which operated the Tornado from Coningsby and which continued to provide pilots for the BBMF following the departure of the Phantoms.

RN-S For the 1994 display season, P7350 appeared in the markings previously carried by another presentation aircraft, in this case Spitfire Mk.IIA, P7832 'Enniskillen' of 72 Squadron, which was one of 17 aircraft presented by the *Belfast Telegraph*'s Spitfire Fund, each of which was named after a province in Northern Ireland. It was entirely appropriate to select an aircraft of 72 Squadron, which today serves at Aldergrove in Northern Ireland, operating the Westland Wessex HC.2 helicopter.

In a slight change to the normal pattern of changing the squadron markings when the aircraft undergo major servicing, after only one season as 'Enniskillen', P7350 went to St Athan for major servicing over the winter of 1994-95, and despite being fully paint stripped and repainted, it was returned to its 72 Squadron markings which were felt to be more appropriate for the aircraft to carry in the year that would mark the 50th anniversary of VE Day. An alternative colour scheme to depict an air-sea rescue Spitfire of Coastal Command was also under consideration.

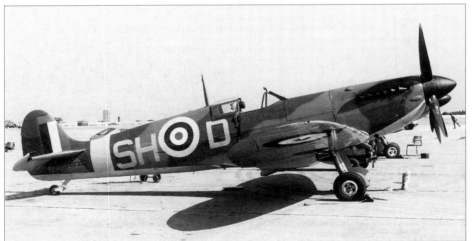

EB-Z In 1985 the Royal Observer Corps celebrated its 60th anniversary and P7350 was repainted to depict a Spitfire Mk.II, P7666, of 41 Squadron which was a presentation aircraft sponsored by the Corps.

UO-T As the Flight's only aircraft which served operationally during the Battle of Britain, for the 1989 display season P7350

once again donned its original 266 (Rhodesia) Squadron codes 'UO-T' in preparation for the celebrations to mark the 50th anniversary of the Battle of Britain, which took place the following year.

YT-F Having depicted the markings of the Coningsby McDonnell Douglas Phantom reserve squadron in 1982, from 1991 P7350

Film appearances: Like the other aircraft of the BBMF used in the film *The Battle of Britain*, P7350 carried a variety of serial numbers, including: N3310; N3312; N3317; N3321 and code letters : 'AI-A'; 'AI-E'; 'BO-H', 'CD-C'; 'CD-M'; 'DO-M'; 'EI-C'.

Spitfire Mk.VB AB910

QJ-J The code letters 'QJ-J' depict a Spitfire of 92 Squadron as operated from Pembrey, Carmarthen, and then Biggin Hill, Kent. First applied to the aircraft when it was owned by Vickers-Armstrongs Ltd and flown by Jeffrey Quill, AB910 carried these code letters painted in a 'thin' style up to the time it was used during the making of the film *The Battle of Britain*.

SO-T After its participation in the Battle of Britain film, AB910 was sent from Coltishall to 5 MU at Kemble for servicing and repainting between 6th March and 28th April 1969, whereupon it returned sporting the code letters 'PB-T', which had been wrongly applied to depict the intended squadron, 145. At that time 145 Squadron was the reserve squadron number allocated to the Lightnings of 226 OCU at Coltishall, and the squadron codes were quickly changed to the correct 'SO-T'.

QJ-J When AB910 was repainted for the 1973 display season, the code letters 'QJ-J' were once again applied to the aircraft, but this time painted in the 'thick' style, which was what it carried when badly damaged in an accident at Bex, Switzerland, on 21st August 1978.

AB910 took on Royal Auxiliary Air Force colours following major repair at Abingdon in 1981, seen here in 1985. MAP

Carrying the legend 'In Memory of R J Mitchell', AB910 in 457 Squadron colours, 1988. MAP

Cranfield, after which it emerged in the markings of 457 (RAAF) Squadron, to represent Spitfire X4936, one of five aircraft presented by the American Heart Foundation which carried the inscription 'In Memory of R J Mitchell'. Whilst the precise details of the inscription were not known, it was decided to depict this particular aircraft as a mark of respect to R J Mitchell, the designer of the Spitfire, who had died on 11th June 1937 at the age of 42. The prototype Spitfire made its first flight on 5th March 1936, almost 50 years to the day before AB910 returned to Coningsby in its new colours.

EB-J For the 1990 season, AB910 was painted in the markings carried by the aircraft of 41 Squadron during the Battle of Britain, and the inscription 'The Guinea Pig Club' in honour of the 647 men treated with the plastic surgery techniques pioneered at East Grinstead by Sir Archibald McIndoe.

MD-E The winter of 1990-91 saw AB910 return again to Cranfield for major servicing, after which it was painted in the colourful markings of 133 (Eagle) Squadron, in which guise it first flew in April 1991.

AE-H It was next the turn of a Canadian squadron to be depicted in the markings carried by AB910, which was repainted over the winter of 1993-94 to represent an aircraft of 402 (RCAF) Squadron as it was marked on D-Day, the 6th June 1944. The code letters 'AE-H' were partially obscured by the black and white fuselage bands painted on all Allied aircraft as a recognition feature. A Canadian maple leaf emblem was painted forward of the cockpit.

XT-M After its accident in Switzerland, AB910 was repaired at Abingdon, Oxfordshire, and repainted at Kemble, arriving back at Coningsby on 23rd October 1981 painted in the code letters 'XT-M' to commemorate 603 (City of Edinburgh) Squadron, Royal Auxiliary Air Force, and the RAuxAF as a whole. The specific markings depicted were the codes formerly carried on two aircraft, L1021 and X4277, both of which were shot down whilst being flown by Flying Officer Richard Hillary, later to become famous as the author of *The Last*

Enemy. When shot down in X4277 on 3rd September, 1940, Hillary was badly burnt but he recovered only to lose his life in a night flying accident in January 1943. These code letters would have been more appropriate if applied to the BBMF's Spitfire Mk.IIA, P7350, which actually served on 603 Squadron and carried the 'XT-' code operationally.

BP-O Between 5th September 1985 and 7th March 1986, AB910 underwent major servicing with the College of Aeronautics at

Film appearances: AB910 also appeared in *The Battle of Britain* film carrying a variety of markings, including: serial numbers N3318; N3319; N3321; N3322 and code letters: 'AI-D'; 'AI-J'; 'AI-M'; 'AI-N'; 'CD-K'.

Spitfire Mk.XIX PM631

Prior to its arrival on the Flight, PM631 operated in the overall silver colour scheme of the THUM Flight. Whilst operated with the Flight from 1957 to the start of filming of the Battle of Britain film in 1967, PM631 flew in a basic camouflage colour scheme without any squadron code letters.

CA-D After its participation in *The Battle of Britain* film, PM631 was repainted in a 1944-style camouflage scheme and the code letters 'CA-D', which were suggested by the staff at HQ Fighter Command to represent an aircraft of 11 Squadron.

DL-E For the 1984 display season PM631 was repainted in the markings carried by a Spitfire Mk.XIV of 91 Squadron at the time of the D-Day landings in June 1944, including the so-called black and white 'invasion stripes' which were painted on the wings and fuselage. Whilst carrying these markings PM631, together with Hurricane LF363 and Lancaster PA474, flew over the D-Day beaches on 6th June 1984, to commemorate the 40th anniversary of the landings. The markings were still on PM631 when, on 5th March 1986, it became the first Spitfire to fly over the City of London since the accident involving SL574 in September 1959, in a flight to mark the 50th anniversary of the first flight of the Spitfire.

PR Mk.XIX PM631 adopted D-Day stripes for the 40th anniversary, 1984. MAP

Highly emphasised name and SEAC colours on PM631, September 1990. MAP

PM631 was also a 'star' of *The Battle of Britain*, seen here as 'N3316' 'DO-G'. Robert Rudhall collection

C During its major serving over the winter of 1989-90, PM631 was serviced by the College of Aeronautics at Cranfield where it was painted by Rogers Aviation in the colours of South-East Asia Command, to once again represent an aircraft of 11 Squadron operating in that theatre, named 'Mary'. The aircraft returned to Coningsby in these colours after a successful test flight from Cranfield on 10th April 1990.

Film appearances: PM631 also flew in *The Battle of Britain* film carrying a variety of markings, including serial numbers N3316; N3317; N3318; N3320 and the code letters 'AI-L'; 'CD-K'; 'DO-G'; 'DO-N'.

Spitfire Mk.XIX PS853

Before its arrival with the Historic Aircraft Flight in 1957, PS853 carried the overall silver colour scheme of the THUM Flight. The aircraft was then painted in camouflage colours, which it carried during its period of

The earliest code markings applied to PS853 were 'ZP-A' of 74 Squadron by 1972.
Neville Franklin collection

service with the Central Fighter Establishment (CFE) at West Raynham, Norfolk, and Binbrook, Lincolnshire. On rejoining the Flight in 1964, PS853 remained in its camouflage colours from its days with the CFE, without the addition of squadron codes. Even after being repainted following use in the film *Battle of Britain*, PS853 was not immediately given squadron code letters.

ZP-A By at least 1972, however, the code letters of 74 Squadron had been applied to PS853.

PR Blue At the suggestion of the Chief of the Air Staff, Air Chief Marshal Sir Andrew Humphrey, PS853 was repainted in the overall blue applied to the high altitude photographic reconnaissance Spitfires. The work was carried out at Kemble over the winter of 1973-74, and the aircraft was returned to Coltishall. However, matt paints were used for the work, and these were found to absorb oil and be very difficult to keep clean, so the aircraft was returned to Kemble later in 1974 and repainted in gloss finish. PS853 still retained these colours in 1980 when it was grounded as a result of problems with its Griffon engine.

PR Blue, code C Following its return to the air after conversion to the Griffon 58 engine from the Shackleton, PS853 was repainted for the 1990 display season, once again in the light blue colours applied to the PR Spitfires. The markings were those of 16 Squadron, which operated PS853 during 1945 and 1946 as part of the 2nd Tactical Air Force (2nd TAF) and later the British Air Forces of Occupation (BAFO). PS853 was wearing these colours when it was offered for sale in November 1994.

Film appearances: The markings carried by PS853 during the Battle of Britain film included: N3316; N3319; N3321 and codes 'AI-G'; 'AI-M'; 'EI-K'.

Spitfire Mk.XIX PS915

Before joining the BBMF permanently in 1987, PS915 carried the silver colour scheme of the THUM Flight, before being painted in camouflage colours for its many years as a gate guardian at West Malling, Kent, Leuchars, Fife, and Brawdy, Dyfed. The aircraft was in camouflage colours when it was collected by British Aerospace in 1984 for restoration to flying condition.

PR blue On delivery to Coningsby in 1987, PS915 carried the standard overall blue finish applied to the RAF's photographic reconnaissance aircraft.

Prototype marks Following major servicing by Lovaux at Bournemouth over the winter of 1991-92, PS915 was painted in the striking prototype colour scheme of camouflaged upper surfaces and yellow undersides with the yellow P in a circle on the fuselage sides. These markings denote a prototype aircraft – in this case the first Spitfire Mk.XIV, JF319. The colour scheme was devised to commemorate the work of the many test pilots who had been involved in the development of the entire Supermarine Spitfire line.

Perhaps the most novel of all markings so far applied to an aircraft of the BBMF, PS915 in the guise of the prototype Mk.XIV, with the famous 'circle-P' symbol on the fuselage, 1993. MAP

Film appearances: PS915 was used in the Battle of Britain film, but as a static exhibit only. In this guise, it carried the serial number N3328 and the code letters 'AI-R'.

Lancaster Mk.I PA474

PA474 did not join the BBMF until 1973, and prior to this had led an interesting and diverse life, firstly as a photographic reconnaissance aircraft with 82 squadron at Benson, and then as a trials aircraft with the College of Aeronautics at Cranfield. After allocation for preservation, PA474 was painted in camouflage colours and placed in storage at Henlow to await the opening of the RAF Museum.

KM-B The code letters KM-B were first applied to the Lancaster at Waddington in 1965 to commemorate the aircraft in which Squadron Leader John Nettleton was awarded the Victoria Cross following a raid by 44 and 97 Squadrons on Augsburg in April 1942. These markings remained on the aircraft until 1979, and were displayed in at least two different styles. When PA474 was adopted by the City of Lincoln, the City's Coat of Arms and the inscription 'City of Lincoln' were applied to the nose of the aircraft below the left hand cockpit window. For a very short time in March 1976, just after the BBMF moved to Coningsby, PA474 was used in a French TV film *Lieutenant Karl*, for which the codes 'KM-B' were carefully adapted to 'KM-F'.

AJ-G As a result of extensive structural repairs which saw the Lancaster grounded throughout 1978, following the 1979 display season it was sent to Lyneham where it was repainted with the code letters 'AJ-G' carried by Lancaster ED932/G of 617 Squadron, flown by Wing Commander Guy Gibson on the 'Dam Busters' raid in May 1943.

SR-D Having undergone its final major servicing at Kemble over the winter of 1983-84, PA474 was repainted as 'SR-D' to depict an aircraft of 101 Squadron, 1 Group, Bomber Command based at Ludford Magna, Lincolnshire, during the Second World War. The choice of squadron was driven by the desire to select one that served with a Group other than 5, and one that was still in current service.

PM-M2 When PA474 was next due major servicing the work was contracted out to West Country Air Services at Exeter, Devon, and when it returned to Coningsby on 17th March 1988, the Lancaster was resplendent in the markings of 103 Squadron, which was based at Elsham Wolds, Lincolnshire. The markings depict Lancaster ED888 which flew 140 operations in its career with both 103 and 576 Squadrons, more than any other Lancaster. Because of the huge array of operations symbols carried on the nose of the aircraft it was necessary for the 'City of Lincoln' Coat of Arms and inscription to be reduced in size and moved further forward on the fuselage side.

WS-J With the frequency of its major servicing extended to six years, it was not until the winter of 1993-94 that PA474 was next repainted. This work was carried out at St Athan, which won the contract in competition with industry. The distinctive markings chosen for the aircraft depict the Bardney, Lincolnshire, based Lancaster W4964, coded 'WS-J' of 9 Squadron, which on its 100th operation dropped a TALLBOY bomb on the German warship *Tirpitz* in Alten Fjord, Norway, on 15th September 1944. PA474 carries the original aircraft's Johnnie Walker nose art and the inscription 'Still Going Strong'.

Unfortunately, the size of the colourful markings to be carried by the aircraft necessitated that the City of Lincoln Coat of Arms and inscription be placed on the other side of the fuselage.

Dakota III ZA947

Before joining the BBMF, ZA947 served with the Royal Aircraft Establishment, later the Defence Research Agency, firstly marked as KG661 and then as ZA947. At first painted in the white and grey colours of the RAE, the Dakota was later finished in the red, white and blue 'raspberry ripple', colours that became the fleet standard for the RAE.

YS-DM Having been allocated to the BBMF for a two-year trial period, ZA947 was sent to Air Atlantique at Coventry Airport, Warwickshire, for major servicing, during which the fabric on the control surfaces was renewed. The aircraft was then flown to Marham, Norfolk, in June 1993 where it was repainted in the camouflage colours of 217 Squadron at the time of Operation MARKET, the airborne attack on Arnhem in September 1944. The markings were chosen to depict the aircraft flown by Flight Lieutenant David Lord who was shot down during the operation on 19th September and killed. His gallantry was subsequently recognised with the posthumous award of the Victoria Cross.

Opposite:

Top: **Spitfire Mk.VB AB910 at the time of filming The Battle of Britain.**
Neville Franklin collection

Bottom left: **When repainted in 1969, Spitfire Mk.IIA P7350 carried the slightly inappropriate codes 'ZH-T' of 266 (Rhodesia) Squadron. 'ZH-' was used by the unit when it flew Hawker Typhoons.** MAP

Bottom Right: **In keeping with the tradition of adopting wartime codes letters of the reserve squadron number allocated to the BBMF's OCU colleagues at both Coltishall and Coningsby, P7350 took the markings of 65 (East India) Squadron from 1991.** MAP

Following is major service 1983-84, PA474 took on 101 Squadron codes. MAP

With the adoption of 103 Squadron markings for 1987-88, PA474 saw its 'City of Lincoln' heraldry reduced in size and moved forward on the fuselage side to accommodate the array of sortie 'scores' carried by the original aircraft. MAP

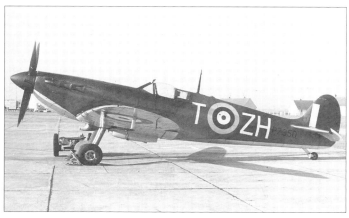